TELLURIDE
HIKING GUIDE

SUSAN KE[

wayfinder PRESS

Ridgway, Colorado

PUBLISHED BY WAYFINDER PRESS
POST OFFICE BOX 217
RIDGWAY, COLORADO 81432
EDITOR/PUBLISHER, MARCUS WILSON

DESIGN AND TYPOGRAPHY BY
PAT WILSON, COUNTRY GRAPHICS, RIDGWAY, CO

PRINTED BY COUNTRY GRAPHICS, RIDGWAY, CO

COVER PHOTOS:
FRONT - BRIDAL VEIL FALLS, GARY ESCHMAN
BACK - *TELLURIDE,* LINDE WAIDHOFER
        SUSAN AND BILL KEES, CHARLES FAZIO

ISBN 0-943727-14-6

Dedicated to my husband, Bill and children, Scott, Lorraine and Blake.

Acknowledgments

Everyone has a story about coming to Telluride. We came from California. Dazed by idealism and shattered dreams of the 1960s, we piled our kids into the Toyota station wagon in the summer of 1972 and drove on all the back roads we could find from Southern California to Telluride. The Ophir wall and the "jewel box," a commonly used reference to night-time Telluride, jumped out at us as we drove into town and parked in front of the Roma Bar.

It was close to midnight; Ed got up from his barstool and greeted us. "Let me buy you a drink. You're the kind of people we want to have in this town," he said. Afterward, feeling certain we had found Utopia, we drove out to the end of the valley and tossed our sleeping bags and pads on the ground outside the car. We slept well that night, awakened early by the sounds of passing trucks. Much to our surprise, we had camped in the parking lot of the Idarado Mine.

At that time, most of the houses and buildings in Telluride had boarded windows. Tumbleweeds blew across the deserted streets providing entertainment for the town's 600 inhabitants. When the walks around town became too familiar, I started to take one step at a time away from the town's perimeter.

Hiking has been a steadily increasing activity over the years for me. Eventually, I covered a lot of territory. My husband's encouragement helped me continue to explore. In innocence and ignorance, I left the house unprepared and was rained, hailed, and snowed upon. I got lost many times, but I finally learned to go prepared for all conditions. Today, my hiking is limited due to bad knees. I am extremely selective about my hikes and I walk with ski poles to deflect the pressure from my knees, but hiking in general has added another dimension to a very full life.

I want to thank my husband for helping me to be prepared outdoors and to understand the meaning of effort. Thank you, Bill Kees, for all you have shared and taught me; you are the hero of my heart. And to my children: Lorraine, for all your hard work typing, editing, and helping me with the computer, neither edition would have appeared without your help; Scott, for your persistence in showing me what it means to work hard to achieve your goals; Blake, for your unfailing positive attitude, and your ability to dream. Thanks to each of you for hiking, counseling, supporting, and loving me, and for being my best friends; I am grateful for the gifts you each have given me. It is to my husband and children that I dedicate this work.

I also pay homage to the Spaniards, the Utes, the miners, and the mountaineers who pioneered the peaks and passes of these mountains, and to the old timers and their families who shared stories with me. In particular, to Mel Griffiths, a good friend and San Juan Mountaineer, who, along with my husband and David Lavender, encouraged me to write and to share what I have learned on these trails. A special thanks to Clay Wadman for his great map work and to Rich Salem, my good friend and neighbor who has helped me overcome a serious computer paranoia, and who considerately and tirelessly took the time to read and to help me organize this writing. Because of his help, this is a manuscript that I am proud to present.

Thanks to all of my very dear hiking friends who got out there, got lost, helped me read the maps and figure out where we were or weren't. My friends have each endured the hardships of getting lost with me and the frustrations of dealing with my fears of exposure and high places, and they have held my hand when I was scared and wimpy. A hearty THANKS to each of you, whose encouragement and inspiration have nurtured my dreams. For without you, I would never have begun this forever unfinished work.

In this edition, I want to attempt to individually thank everyone who has taken the time to share books, photos, and stories with me. I have hiked and spoken with people for more than a quarter of a century now, and I may have unintentionally omitted some. I sincerely apologize for any omissions. Some on this list have died and some may have forgotten their contribution, but I wish to extend recognition to those whose help has been invaluable:

Minnie Ackerman
Denise Adams
Jerry Albin
Kirk Alexander
Ron Allred
Mary Baker
Harold Ballard
John Ballard
Gary and Claire Bennett
Fred Blackburn
Sylvia Blackburn
Cathy Bowers
Mary Boyer
Buffalo Girls
George and Gay Cappis
Midge and Bud Carrier
Alta Cassietto
Terry Catsman
Albina Clementi
Sally Cole
Cleona Crozier
Norman Dally
Jim and Agatha Dalpez
Pat Daniels
Dick DePagter
Doyle and Betty Ruth Duncan
Bill Dunkelberger
Dale and Bonnie Dyer
Sky Fairlamb
Charles Fazio

Donna and Terry Fernald
Frances Frank
Beth Gage
Cecil and Francis Goldsworthy
Mel Griffiths
Tom and Rena Hedlund
Kim Hilbert
Lillian Huff
Clinton Impson
Ethel Jackson
Cathy James
Mike Kimball
Lucille (Rogers) Knox
David Lavender
Billy Mahoney
Susie Mansfield
Mouse McDonald
Charlie McKnight
Beverly McTigue
Chris Newman
Don and Frances O'Rourke
Donald O'Rourke, Jr.
Jerry and Dawna O'Rourke
Al Norris
Don Oberto
Carrie Parmentier
Leighton and Marina Patterson
Jack and Davine Pera
Howard Ramsey
Catherine Reece

Dennis Reece
Arlene Reid
Susan Ritchey
Sherry Rose
Dave Rote
Rich Salem
Andrew Sawyer
Joan Schmitz
Bucky and Pat Schuler
Janice Simpson
Joe Smart
Norman Squire
Johnny Stevens
Larry Stevens
Alice Taylor
Francis Vella
Esther Taylor
Irene Visintin
Clay Wadman
Paul Weissman
Priscilla Wells
Francis Werner
Steve West
Mona Wilcox
Larry Wilkinson
Alice Williams
Jo Wilson
Doug and Lauren Wolfe
Harry and Marie Wright
Elvira Wunderlich
Virginia Brown Zunich

Contents

HIKES IN LIZARD HEAD WILDERNESS

HIKES EAST OF TELLURIDE

OTHER HIKES OF INTEREST

TELLURIDE SKI AREA HIKES

Introduction

Telluride is nestled in a box canyon at 8,745 feet in the wings of the San Juan Mountain Range, a rugged landscape where the lure of fortune summoned many. The natural beauty of the Telluride area beckons those who come and stay, but few pass farther than the front doors.

The San Juans are a spectacular range, speckled with abandoned mines, mills, tramways, railroad rights-of-way, and multi-colored rock. The mountains around Telluride offer awe-inspiring terrain, rich in historical lore. No other range in the continental United States has as much land above 10,000 feet as the San Juans. The mining districts alone cover 4,891 square miles. The mountain passes are high and often inaccessible, yet hardy gold and silver seekers braved the elements to build supply roads.

Snuggled among the mighty and mystical San Juan Mountains is the town of Telluride. Once known as the City of Gold, Telluride is now a National Historic District. Old homes, churches, a cemetery, an old brick school building, and a courthouse preserve the flavor of earlier times. Visit the museum at the top of North Fir Street to view photos and artifacts of yesteryear.

When the Spanish explorers came through in the late 1700s, they named many prominent features of the area. In the 1800s, the area was sparsely populated by fur traders and Ute Indians. In 1873, the Utes relinquished their mineral rights. Some say that they left a curse when they left the area in 1877.

In the 1890s, the miners created a civilization here, and their remnants are today's testimonial to the triumphs and tribulations of an era vanished but not vanquished. The miners were tough; traversing steep trails on strikingly rugged and vertical terrain to work in the high mountain basins. The life expectancy of men who worked in the mines was much shorter than it is today. Then, old age came at thirty-five.

San Juan Mountain people were persevering. There was no stigma attached to failure; the only failure was not to try. Many left the valley, certain they were victims of the Ute curse. There were no neutral moments in the mining camps where the threat of tragedy was always present. The immigrants who had risked everything to get here and those who stayed were incredibly optimistic and hearty.

Once known as San Miguel City and Columbia, Telluride has a rich and diversified history. At the turn of the century, Telluride was sophisticated and prosperous, and mining activities punctuated the town's character. Perhaps the high-risk mentality of the valley's surrounding mining camps set the tone, laying the groundwork for the excitement and high energy found here today.

Telluride has always attracted visionaries. Today, with a keen understanding of the relationship of man to land, the San Miguel Land Trust, a non profit organization dedicated to preserving land in its natural state, has had the vision and the perserverance to buy Bear Creek to protect for eternity

Exploring this region provides rich rewards. Perhaps as in nature itself, with its abbreviated springs and summers and the protracted winters, the urgency of enjoying the moment is apparent. However, there is more than spectacular scenery here. Take the time to savor the spirit, to be totally sensitized, and to listen to the echoes of history while passing the remnants of days gone by. Your footsteps are added to those who came before you. People with different outlooks, ambitions, and philosophies have left their blood, sweat, and tears. While you walk and look at these vast vistas, keep in mind that these mountains have experienced throbbing, thriving life. The mountainscapes you see as untouched have all been beloved manuscripts of previous generations.

Part of the fiber of our present existence is found in the history of those who came before us. Most of the experience of the Spaniards and the Utes has been lost. We don't know much about what happened. Much of the history of the San Juans is documented with words such as "supposedly" and "reportedly" and has been communicated from secondary sources. This guide relates some of the lore and legendary mystique of the basins and valleys around Telluride while pointing you toward the trails. Many of these stories are based on personal interviews with old timers and popular legend. This history begins with the miners. We know little about those who populated the region before.

The challenge is to retain the little we do know. Looking at the ski area hillside above town, you'd hardly know it had once been clear cut. So often vision is limited by a narrow view of the present. It is easy to forget the dreams of others who came before. Love and enjoy what is here now as you take the time to understand and to appreciate the evolution. It is easy to ignore changes as they occur right before your eyes.

This guide is an aid to those who want a helping hand. It is an introduction to the mystery and the magic of the mountains around Telluride, intended to help you find the paths pioneered by mules and miners in search of silver and gold. It is a general guide and is no substitute for common sense. You are responsible for yourself out there, so be prepared and take precautions.

Writing this second edition has been even more challenging than the first. Then, I was overjoyed giving people directions to the spectacular sights around the Telluride valley and seeing the hikes bound inside a book cover. My original intent was to describe the hikes which originated in the town or the valley and to take you on trails which circled the town of Telluride. Now, I want to take you further, to give you a taste of the surrounding areas where shepherds herded and other mining communities existed. I feel a greater responsibility to improve, to refine, and to expand. This work is growing into a life project. The farther I hike, the further I want to go.

Hiking Hints and Safety

Please keep in mind when following this guide that the trails may vary occasionally from the descriptions and directions given. Overall, those variations will not usually significantly alter the route, however, in some cases it will. The trails continue to change as natural forces, increased usage, and the work of the U.S. Forest Service impact the terrain. Winter snowfalls, avalanches and fallen debris leave their impact on the trails. The U.S. Forest Service and volunteers clean up and improve their paths. Deer and elk roam while more people traipse through the woods. Be aware and pay attention. Always know where you are when hiking in the mountains. Plan your route in more detail before attempting a particular hike. Be aware that this book is merely a general guide, not a precise, scientific document.

Trail safety requires advance preparation and common sense. Bring waterproof matches or a lighter, a candle, and a headlamp or flashlight, food, water, warm clothing, a wool hat and gloves, rain gear, first-aid supplies, a map, a compass, a whistle, and a companion. Always tell someone else where you are going.

The **difficulty** ratings of easy, moderate, difficult, or extremely difficult are relative. They are based on elevation gain, time, trail condition, and my own subjective calculations. If you have come from your desk at sea level, go slowly and assess your fitness. The difficulty varies with fitness as well. I am well over 55 years old. I walk at a moderate, steady pace. I have lived in Telluride for a quarter of a century and I am usually acclimatized.

The **maps** given are general guidelines. Use U.S.G.S. or *Trails Illustrated Topo* maps for accuracy and a perspective of the surrounding areas. Note the distinction between Forest Service trails and others. Many of the trails found in the Forest Service system have been improved and are maintained. Stay off private land and be respectful and considerate of landholders, miners, and the mountains. Many of the trails cross private property where permission is required to enter.

The **distances** are identified as one way or round trip. It is difficult to be extremely accurate. They were measured by hand on topographic maps, and you must allow for error.

The **times** given are a general calculation for the average hiker who will take few and short breaks. They do not include the driving time or time getting to the trailhead. Pay closer attention to the times indicated than the distances. Remember, the times will vary according to your own ability, acclimatization, and fitness. I have tried to approximate general guidelines as a reference, but be aware of variations and plan your day accordingly. You may run or walk faster to make the hiking times shorter, or you may walk slower, stop longer and rest to make them longer. I recommend taking minimal and short breaks. It is difficult to continue after a long break.

The **elevations** are given to help you gauge the degree of difficulty. Remember that all roads lead upward. Beware, for the altitude can take its toll, causing dehydration, headaches, lightheadedness, and extreme fatigue. If you are out of breath with little effort below 10,000 feet, you are not ready for the longer hikes described. If you have high blood pressure or heart problems, consult your doctor before embarking on any of these hikes; in addition, confine your hiking to the easier and the lower hikes.

Clothing should be layered. No matter how warm it looks when you start, be prepared for change. With adequate layering you can stay warm and prevent hypothermia, the condition of extreme cooling of the body's core temperature. I recommend using a day pack for your comfort. (It is possible to backpack and to spend the night in many places, doing these hikes at a more leisurely pace. However, I have written this guide with the day hiker in mind.) For those in good health who have difficulty, rest, water, and a leisurely pace should alleviate problems.

Your **safety** is important. Hike in groups of three or more. If someone gets hurt, one person should seek help while the other stays with the victim. Don't get lost. Keep your group together and pay attention to prominent terrain features. Know how to use a compass and a map. I have worked hard to accurately describe the trails, but there may be errors. (If you find descriptions misleading or inaccurate, or if you note a helpful addition, please contact me or the publisher to clarify or correct.) Get an early start to cross passes and reach maximum elevations before noon to avoid lightning storms which often occur after mid-day. Purchase a Hiking Certificate for back country search and rescue—it covers the cost of rescue and immediate first aid initiated through the local sheriff's office, in the unlikely event of an accident. This may be purchased through the Colorado Division of Wildlife, 6060 Broadway, Denver, Colorado 80216 or at Telluride Sports.

Campfires can cause extreme destruction and harm. Check with the BLM or the Forest Service to find out whether fires are pernmitted. Please use caution. If you camp overnight and use a fire, follow these guidelines: Never leave your campsite or go to bed before your campfire is completely out. Use dirt and water and stir it up to make sure the embers are cold to the touch before leaving. Smoke only while stopped somewhere free of flammable materials and pick up your butts. Use existing fire rings wherever possible. In pristine areas away from rivers and creeks, build your fire in a fire pan and elevate the pan off the ground. Completely scatter the ashes and small coals away from the campsite where they won't be noticed.

Good **health** and respecting the environment are essential. Do not drink the water from streams which seem inviting but may be contaminated. Carry your own water or purify with a filter or other purification system. Giardia, an intestinal parasite, is widespread in these mountains and can cause severe illness. Bring a minimum of one quart of water per person per day. If you must use toilet paper, get at least 100 feet off the trail and burn and bury all waste at least eight inches deep. PLEASE DO NOT LITTER.

Trail **etiquette** requires consideration of others, respect, and remembering that you are a guest. Where horses are allowed, they have the right-of-way. Stand off the trail until the horse passes. Do not take shortcuts. Switchbacks help prevent trail erosion. Dogs disturb wildlife and are best left at home. Preserve the public's right to access trails by cooperating with private landowner requests. PACK OUT YOUR TRASH.

Some **ski area sites** are described because they offer relatively easy, scenic and historic routes. The ski area is an integral part of the town's recent development, and many of the ski runs were named after mining claims. Motorcycles and dogs are not permitted on the ski area, but bicycles are allowed. Go at your own risk and pay attention.

Overall, the percentage of people who experience severe problems is relatively small. Get out there and have an exhilarating, awesome experience to add to those miraculous, meaningful, and memorable moments in life.

HAVE FUN AND RESPECT THE MOUNTAINS!

Beyond Hiking

Besides hiking there are other summer, spring, and fall activities to pursue in the area. Trout fishing, mountain biking, rock climbing, rafting, hang gliding and bird watching are among the many available endeavors. If you are looking for **places to camp**, you might try the following:

Telluride Town Park: East edge of town, on the San Miguel River. Toilets, showers, water, picnic tables and fire pits. Elevation: 8,770 feet.

Ilium Valley: Five miles west of Telluride on "National Forest Access, South Fork Road, Ilium." Elevation: approximately 8,500 feet.

Alta Lakes: Approximately ten miles south of Telluride, turn left onto "National Forest Access, Boomerang Road, Alta Lakes." Drive five miles to the ghost town of Alta and another 1/2 mile to the campground at the Lakes. Tables, fireplaces. Good fishing. Elevation: 11,250 feet.

Sunshine Campground: Off Highway 145, approximately seven miles south of Telluride. Toilets, tables, fireplaces. Elevation: 9,560 feet.

Matterhorn Campground: Approximately twelve miles south of Telluride, before Trout Lake. Toilets, tables, fireplaces. Elevation: 9,480 feet.

Woods Lake: Nine miles west of Telluride off Highway 145 on Fall Creek Road. Toilets. Elevation: 9,420 feet.

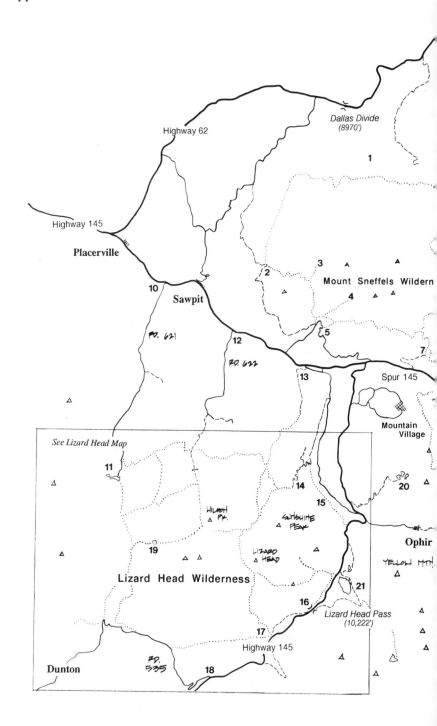

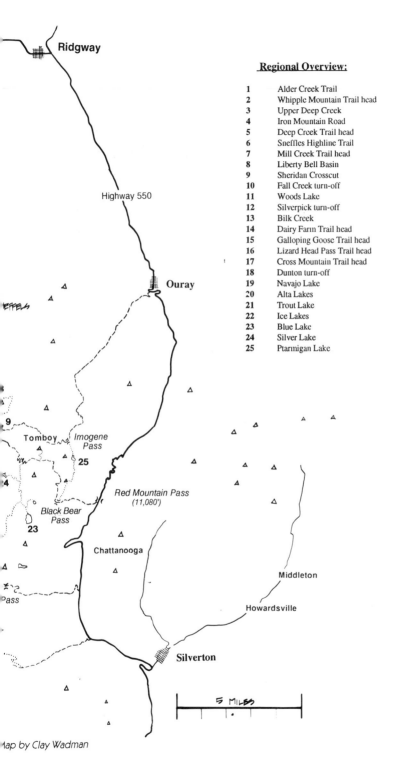

Regional Overview:

1	Alder Creek Trail
2	Whipple Mountain Trail head
3	Upper Deep Creek
4	Iron Mountain Road
5	Deep Creek Trail head
6	Sneffles Highline Trail
7	Mill Creek Trail head
8	Liberty Bell Basin
9	Sheridan Crosscut
10	Fall Creek turn-off
11	Woods Lake
12	Silverpick turn-off
13	Bilk Creek
14	Dairy Farm Trail head
15	Galloping Goose Trail head
16	Lizard Head Pass Trail head
17	Cross Mountain Trail head
18	Dunton turn-off
19	Navajo Lake
20	Alta Lakes
21	Trout Lake
22	Ice Lakes
23	Blue Lake
24	Silver Lake
25	Ptarmigan Lake

Ridgway

Highway 550

Ouray

Tomboy   Imogene Pass

25

Red Mountain Pass
(11,080')

Black Bear Pass

23

Chattanooga

Middleton

Howardsville

Silverton

5 MILES

Map by Clay Wadman

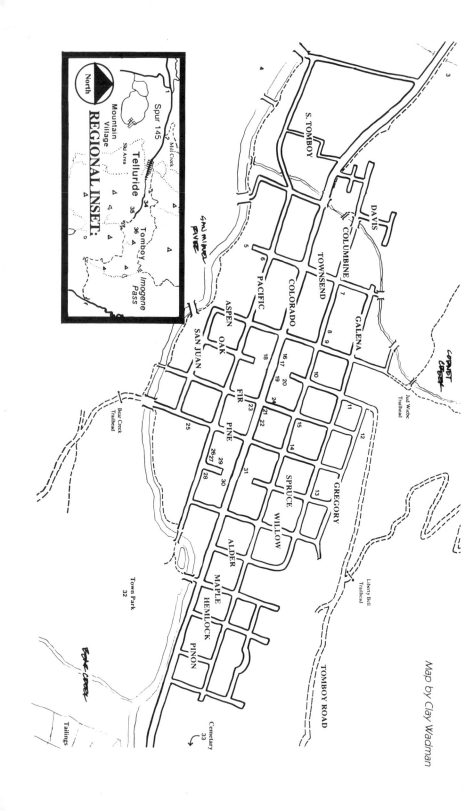

Map by Clay Wadman

Walks Around Town

Orient yourself to the area and the altitude by staying on the valley floor before you begin your ascent to the basins above. The sites and the walks below may be helpful in assessing your fitness and readiness for more.

Bike Path:
A. The Town of Telluride took possession of the spur, this portion of Highway 145 from the state of Colorado, and created this well used trail where walkers, joggers, runners, bikers, strollers, and skaters enjoy much time.

B. San Miguel City (just off the bike path, across from the gas station)

C. Society Turn

River Trail:
Presently, this runs from the town park to the Coonskin lift, and then continues along the river to Boomerang Road, just opposite the gas station. The section of the trail from Boomerang to Coonskin was dedicated to Helen Newell who once walked or skied the trail daily from her Gold King condominium and picked up trash. Helen's love of the outdoors and her desire to preserve open space were an inspiration to many. Eventually, this trail will be extended to meet with the bike path at Society Turn. The creation of this trail represents a tremendous cooperative effort between private landowners and government.

After touring the sites below and completing the walks above, these shorter hikes may also be tried:

Galloping Goose
Waterline Trail
Trout Lake railroad grade, from the trestle to Lizard Head
Royer Gulch (often snow-free first in the spring)
Jud Wiebe (go from west to east in the spring)
Hope Lake
Bear Creek
Coonskin
Stillwell Tunnel (above Jud Wiebe on the Liberty Bell trail)

Exercising in Telluride is difficult for those from sea level. Drink lots of water; avoid caffeine and alcohol; pay attention to your body, and rest as often as you need. It is not worth ruining your vacation by pushing too hard the first day. Time at this elevation helps a great deal. I have prepared "Around Town" for your understanding and appreciation of the historical spirit of this region. Spend a few days on the valley floor exploring this beloved local area and adapt to the altitude before you begin hiking at higher elevations. Your enjoyment of hikes above the valley will be enriched.

The past persists in the historical town of Telluride. There were 100 bars when over 5,000 people inhabited Telluride in the mining heyday. The ski area opened in the winter of 1972-73; the first link from the town to the mountain, the Coonskin Lift, was in operation in 1975; and active mining stopped in 1979. Idarado Mining Co. still employs a small number of people for reclamation work and safety. The mining era was an environment of pay dirt, and more than a century of excavation had its impact on the valley. The vestiges of mining activity are extensive. At the northeast end of the valley you can see the mine and mill sites. Above the town park, to the southeast, are the tailings, the residue of mining activity, today covered in grass and supported by an elaborate sprinkler system.

When the miners arrived, the silver veins were rich, and three small communities existed: **Pandora**, at the east end of the valley, **San Miguel City**, on the west side, near today's gas station, and in between was the tent city of **Columbia**. U. S. Postal Service confusion between Columbia, California and Columbia, Colorado, resulted in the name change in 1881, when **Telluride** was established. In 1883, Telluride became the seat of San Miguel County.

The sites and buildings below represent but a minuscule view of the pulsating activity once in town. Parts of some of the stories are told on the plaques around town. Nearly all of the buildings around town could have plaques on them to commemorate our local history. Behind the new facades are the spirited and brave souls of the miners who made their fortunes and met their fates here.

In 1964, Telluride became a National Historic District and is now protected by the Town's Historic Architectural Review Commission. Many of the buildings in this tour have withstood the hardships of aging and have experienced extensive remodeling; some are newly constructed on sites where the original buildings collapsed or were destroyed by fire. As you walk around, please be respectful and considerate of private property and local inhabitants. Remember that people live and work in these places today.

Starting from west to east, the sites below will augment your understanding of the area. For further knowledge, go to the bookstores, the library, and the museum. There is much to learn.

1. **Society Turn,** at one time hosting a "Welcome" sign, is located at the west end of the valley where Highway 145 meets the spur. In the 1930s the Telluride Golf Club was located across the highway at the bottom of Lawson Hill in the flat area by the river. Teens enjoyed many a good time at beach parties there. In 1995, when this spur was acquired by the Town of Telluride, a bicycle path was constructed. In the mining era, families drove or rode horses out there on Sundays to wave, say hello, picnic and turn around. Hence, the name. This is a wonderful spot for a photo.

The Brewery

2. The **Brown Homestead** is located along the spur of Highway 145 off the bike path across from the gas station. The log remains of the oldest building in the Telluride valley denote the original home of Frank Brown, one of the postmasters of the short-lived **San Miguel City**. Conflicting historical reports indicate anywhere from eleven to three hundred persons resided in San Miguel City.

3. **The Telluride Brewery** existed on the terraced hillside on the west end of town, near the present day middle-high school. Old timers remember enjoying the scenery from beside the ponds, while people ate and sipped beer. The pure and tasty water from Butcher Creek was used to create an outstanding high altitude blend. Howard Ramsey, who left town in 1913, remembers the Brewery fire: "Two lines of people passed buckets back and forth filling them with water while the local kids drank beer."

4. The **town dump** was located where the Coonskin parking area and the Shandoka apartments now stand west of the Coonskin chair lift, #7. In the early 1930s a "shanty town" hosted bums who jumped the railroad cars for transportation in and out of the valley. Dead animals and human refuse festered within town limits as raw sewage and toxic waste ran into the San Miguel River. In 1972, the dump was a favorite spot for treasure seekers who braved the stench and skunk and magpie populations. The section of the river trail there is dedicated to Helen Newell, a longtime local resident who supported open space preservation.

5. **The Telluride Depot,** where the Rio Grande Southern Railroad stopped, is situated at the end of South Townsend. Telluride's narrow gauge railroad arrived in 1891 and operated until 1951. This was a busy area in those years with the hustle and bustle of transportation.

6. **Swede-Finn Hall** is one of the links to ethnicity around town during the mining era. Located at the corner of Townsend and Pacific Streets, it was built for social events; however, liquor was not allowed at the social hall. Cleona Crozier, who graduated from Telluride High in 1924, recounts classmates going on strike for a week after the following incident: "After the dance closed at 11:00 p.m. as required. One boy found a key and let the other students back into the hall to continue the party. When a teacher discovered the students' presence, the teens were sent home and the boy who had the key was to be expelled. Students walked Main Street

Telluride Elementary School

in protest for one week; the administration relented only to serve the protesters with a punishment of giving them a 50% deduction in their grades upon return to school." While everyone of the various nationalities was not restricted to living in any specific area, immigrants had a tendency to habituate and to congregate near those of similar language backgrounds. Swedish and Finnish families occupied the area from Fir Street to the west. Italians lived on East Columbia, and Irish, German, and Tyrolean-Austrian immigrants lived from Oak Street to the cemetery. "Cousin Jacks" were known as some of the world's finest miners from Wales, England and Scotland. To some degree, a stratified class system existed, yet there was a general integration of nationalities in many aspects of life.

7. **Telluride Elementary School** was built in 1896. This was originally the elementary, junior high, and high school. The main floor housed the grade school. Grades 7-12 were upstairs, and the basement held band and shop space. It and the Catholic church are the two oldest buildings in town.

8. The **Pinhead House**, the smaller home, next to L.L.Nunn's larger home, was used to house engineering students from Cornell University who were recruited to work and to study with Nunn. These students were locally referred to as "Pinheads."

9. The **L.L. Nunn House** was built on the corner of Aspen and Columbia Streets in 1887 when Nunn created the world's first alternating current electric power plant. George Westinghouse provided the generators and Nunn sent current two miles away to the Gold King Mine.

10. The big brick building once known as **The Davis House** is located on the corner of Oak Street and Columbia Street and was built in 1894 for E.L.Davis who owned the Mayflower, Nellie, and the Etta gold mines. Davis was an early real estate entrepreneur who served as president of the Telluride Board of Trade. During

Pinhead House

the 1918 flue epidemic, when owned by Dr. Oshner, the house was used for a short time as a hospital.

11. The **Litchfield House** on North Oak Street was built in 1900 and appears in photos of the 1914 flash flood. The house was swept off its foundation and rested at an angle. It is listed in the National Register of Historic Homes. Occupants of this house have reported friendly ghost stories. One tenant was visited by a man who sat at his bedside. Another experienced slammed doors and swinging chandeliers. Still another experienced the turning on and off of an unplugged radio. Some attribute these pranks to Edward, who died in 1913, and may still roam the halls of this house.

12. The **Telluride Historical Museum** at the top of North Fir Street was the old Miner's Hospital, constructed in 1893 by Dr. H.C. Hall. Later, it was known as the Drs. Allen and Hadley's Hospital, and even later as the American Legion Hospital.

13. **St. Patrick's Catholic Church** on the corner of Spruce and Galena Streets was built in 1896. "Catholic Hill" was a popular sledding run through the early 1980s when winter sledding signs were posted to allow safe sledding. A ghost has been reported to reside here.

14. During the miner's strikes in the early 1900s, the militia occupied the hospital and union miners were turned away. The Western Federation of Miner's Union built its own hospital in 1901 at the **Miner's Union Hall** located on the corner of Columbia and Pine Street. This building was originally an Elk's Lodge and later used as a post office. It was also used as a hospital for a few years during the miner's strikes.

Town Hall

15. **Town Hall** on Fir Street and Columbia was the first school in town, built in 1883. The tower was added later to hang and dry fire hoses.

16. The **Galloping Goose** was one of the last narrow gauge railroad vehicles which ran into Telluride. The Goose was a hybrid, a Pierce Arrow bus with a Buick engine built to run on rails. Eight of these were originally built. No. 4 resides in Telluride. It now rests on Colorado Avenue on the west side of the courthouse. Acquired by the Denver and Rio Grande Western Railroad, the Galloping Goose service to Telluride was discontinued and the tracks were torn up in 1951. Old timers remember the scare of

Galloping Goose

riding over the Ophir Loop where the goose swayed on the tracks high above the ground. The train went slowly from Dolores to the top of Lizard Head Pass and passengers remembered holding on to their hats for the scary, speedy descent.

Stories about how the name originated vary. Some credit the goose-like honk of the horn and the waddling gait on uneven track. Others say the name originated from a woman hanging out her laundry, who commented to another that the train looked like a goose, galloping down the track.

Access was always a problem in Telluride. A famous freighter named Dave Wood used mule trains to transport freight to town and the mines above. Miners used the Dave Wood Freight Line to transport ore to Montrose over Horsefly Mesa. Photos of his mules carrying wire cable to the Nellie Mine can be seen at the museum.

Attempts to solve longstanding transportation problems were made in the 1880s by Otto Mears, an enterprising Russian-English orphan-immigrant, who was responsible for building the "Million Dollar Highway," U.S. Highway 550, which runs from Durango to Grand Junction. In 1880, the "Pathfinder of the San Juans," Otto Mears, built a toll road over Dallas Divide from Montrose to Telluride which can be seen today from Highway 62. Mears started the 162 mile narrow gauge system linking Durango, Mancos, Dolores and Stoner that traveled over a wooden trestle at the Ophir Loop where the Goose ran. (Check out the hike/bike trail as well.)

17. This has been the **San Miguel County Courthouse** since 1887. The original courthouse burned down less than two years after it was constructed, and, in 1887, some of the original bricks were used to build the red brick courthouse where the clock tells "Telluride time" today. The stars on the side of the building are ends of tension rods used to give the structure more stability.

18. **Elks Park** is located on Colorado Avenue, across from the courthouse.

San Miguel County Courthouse

Historic plaques and photos here tell stories of the area .

19. East of the courthouse is the **New Sheridan Hotel**, originally built in 1895. In 1897, the first building burned and was rebuilt in 1899. It was renamed the New Sheridan and William Jennings Bryan gave his "Cross of Gold" speech on a platform built in the front of the building. In 1978, scenes from *Butch and Sundance: The Early Years* were filmed here.

New Sheridan

20. **The Opera House** was built in 1914 and has hosted incredible cultural diversity ever since. Until 1951 some of the high school proms were held there. Many graduations were also hosted there until 1996.

21. **The Busy Corner Pharmacy** building was built in 1883. Old timers remember hanging out here at the soda fountain in their teens, slurping "Lucky Mondays." The second floor housed a bowling alley and offices. Later, it became the Telluride Real Estate Company building; it burned down in 1990 and was rebuilt the next year.

22. Robert Leroy Parker, notoriously known as **Butch Cassidy**, reportedly worked in Telluride as an 18 year old mule skinner. Butch also supposedly worked for Jack Elliott who had a meat market in Ophir and ran Log Hotel at Placerville. He was also reported to have worked on a ranch in Norwood. Butch collected $20,000 when he robbed his first bank in Telluride in June of 1889 where San Miguel Valley Bank operated. This site was located where the **Mahr Building** now stands, three buildings east of Fir Street on Colorado Avenue. While leaving the area, Butch's horse went lame and was left behind. A local sheriff later strutted around town on the horse as if he had taken it away from Butch. Subsequently, Butch bought a ranch in Wyoming; some suspect with stolen Telluride bank money. The original bank building eventually burned down in 1890.

23. In 1885, this was the location of the **first courthouse**, built on Colorado Avenue and Fir Street, where the Telluride Sports building now exists.

24. Today's **Free Box**, a concept created by community members in the 1970s, and constructed on Pine Street above the corner on the main street, offers one man's trash as another's treasure. In the early 1970s, a local child got lice from an unwashed shirt, emphasizing the need to purify garments donated. The Telluride tradition of helping one another is represented today in the continued active existence of the free box.

25. The **Pick and Gad** located on South Pine Street was a bordello. Old

timers who remember many of the girls who "worked on the line" recall them as caring, considerate, generous people.

26. By the early 1900s, 24 bordellos were established in town, employing nearly 175 "working women," many of whom had come here by the lure of false promises, without money or income, and were forced into virtual slave labor on the seamy side of town. Suicide, morphine overdose, addiction, and alcoholism were common escapes from the nightmares of their realities. **Popcorn Alley** was the red light district. The name was derived from the incessant slamming of outhouse doors, which sounded like popcorn popping. The bordellos were upstairs and there were restaurants downstairs run by the town's few Chinese immigrants. In the early 1970s, opium paraphernalia was discovered during building renovations. One local found a sign: "No opium smoking allowed." Women who

Popcorn Alley

worked independently used the tiny two room structures known as cribs to entertain and comfort miners. The cribs on Pacific Street were restored in 1983.

27. **The Silver Bell** building, today used as the Ah Haa School, on the corner of Spruce and Pacific Streets, was also a bordello. Supposedly, the ghost of Ramona, who ended her life the day after she turned 21, resides here. During the building's 1985 renovation, her fading photo and a single rose were mysteriously discovered one morning by workers. Generous and big hearted "Big Billie" also worked here and helped many a hungry miner fill his stomach with a good meal.

28. The children's reading room in the **Wilkinson Library**, that stone portion of the building located on Spruce Street and the alley behind Timberline Hardware, was originally built in the 1880s to serve as a jail. When Larry and Betty Wilkinson moved to Telluride in 1970 and found there was no library, they started the Telluride Community Library with volunteer help and donations and worked in conjunction with the Montrose Library and book mobile from 1972-1973. Later, they got a grant through the Park Service and the State Historical Society for $7,500 and restored the jail and moved into it in 1976-1977. The library district serves more than the town, encompassing the same boundaries as the school district. It has grown from volunteer non-profit efforts into a highly technical information center.

29. **The Senate**, originally a two story building, was a bordello on the top and a saloon and gambling hall on the first floor. Jack Dempsey was reported to have washed dishes here. (He also reportedly washed dishes at the Smuggler Mine from which he was fired.) Recently, the local weekly newspaper moved into this building. In the early 1970s, it operated as a fine restaurant and bar. The bullet hole in the floor was made when someone shot off a sheriff's ear. There was a roulette wheel and game table present, and a door broken by the first ski area owner who left the restaurant yelling because he wasn't served right away. The story goes that the disgruntled ski area developer grabbed one of the swinging doors and jumped up and down on it until it ripped off the hinges. This door was later auctioned off as Telluride's "2nd biggest ripoff!" A wicker body basket hung from the ceiling as a reminder of those injured miners carried down from the mines—it must have carried a miner who survived his accident, for those who didn't were buried in the baskets. Often used as a coffin, these baskets are from which the idiom, "basket case," may have originated.

30. **Masonic Lodge** was located above the Timberline Hardware store on Colorado Avenue, and served a fraternal function for miners separated from family members. Fraternal organizations were like family to miners far from home. Scenes from *Butch and Sundance: The Early Years* were also filmed here.

31. **The Roma Bar** contains a "back bar" which dates from the mid 1800s and was transported from Rome, Italy, arriving in town before the railroad. In March of 1940, one of the biggest "high grading" cases in local history was solved when the proprietor of the Roma bar confessed that the miniature mill in the basement was used to grind ore stolen from the mines around Telluride. Later, one of the proprietor's kin became county commissioner and helped stock the high basin lakes with fish as well as instigated the creation of the town park.

32. **Town Park** is today the site of multi-use family activity:

a. **Kids pond-** Huck Finn Day activities are hosted by the Elks who stock this pond. Fishing here is limited to children under twelve. In the early 1970s, my son Scott often caught his limit, which I froze to feed the family in those early lean years in town.

b. **Jail-** This log structure was built in 1878 and used as a jail. It once sat on Colorado Avenue by the courthouse and was replaced by a stone structure, now part of the Wilkinson Library.

c. **Imagination Station-** The play structure was created, built and supported by the volunteer efforts of the community.

d. **Firecracker Hill-** The site of Fourth of July excitement when Telluride firemen set off fireworks displays.

e. **The Beaver Ponds-** Once populated with tail-slapping, wood chewing, log piling mammals whose busy work ethic offered summer evening entertainment for adults and children of town. Trappers kept the beaver population under control before dogs, careless campers, pop shooters, and construction drove them away. The town has recently made efforts to rebuild the beaver population.

33. A walk around the **Lone Tree Cemetery**, located at the east end of town, is worthwhile. Cemetery populations frequently reflect the sociology of an area and a stroll through the Lone Tree Cemetery will reveal interesting statistics about the Telluride region. However, this was not the first cemetery. The first cemetery in this region was located further west, nearer to the first town in the San Miguel Valley, San Miguel City. Unmarked stone-lined grave sites still exist on private property in an aspen grove there. The Lone Tree Cemetery, which is used today, was the second cemetery in the San Miguel Valley.

Between 1880 and 1920, when over 40 million people emigrated to the United States, the mining frontier of the Telluride region evolved into a prosperous community, surrounded by high altitude gold and silver mines. Hard rock mining was the major industry in the region, sup-

Lone Tree Cemetery

ported by merchants, ranchers, and other service providers. The only segregations reflected in the cemetery are found in the Elks burial plot on the south side and the Masons on the east side. Catholics, Protestants and other diverse groups were buried among one another. Tyroleans from the mountains of northern Italy, Swedes and Finns from the Nordic hinterlands, Welsh and Cornishmen, among other nationalities, along with U.S. citizens, lived, worked, played, died and were buried together while creating this intensely diversified community.

The land for the Lone Tree Cemetery was donated approximately 110 years ago by George S. Andrus who interred his two year old son here. This land was earlier known as the St. James Placer, located at 8,800 feet, east of the town of Telluride. A majority of the gravestone's writing faces east, looking toward Ingram and Bridal Veil Falls and the community of Pandora. Lone Tree Cemetery's southern exposure on the gently sloping hillside keeps the grave sites relatively snow free in the winter, a common time of death in the mountains.

Much like the early years in Telluride itself, the Lone Tree Cemetery reflects the unpretentious simplicity of the working class. Many of the coffins were plain wooden boxes. Headstones and burial crypts were generally frugal. Monuments and markers above ground were predominantly granite. Marble was the next most common stone used, generally associated with names of Italian descent.

More than 1,200 are buried with headstones or markers in the Lone Tree Cemetery— twice as many males as females. Epidemics, pneumonia, natural disasters, and mining accidents were common causes of death. Children below the age of ten years account for 25% of those buried. One third of the children died before they reached one year of age. In 1905, diphtheria and scarlet fever epidemics took many lives, and in the winter of 1917, 10% of the population of Telluride died of the flu. Along with many other factors, avalanches and freezing have accounted for the loss of life.

Obituary, August 25, 1899; *Telluride Journal*: "There was an impressive funeral procession that followed the remains of Mabel Walker to the cemetery yesterday. The pallbearers were women. Six of her sisters in shame, tastily attired in modest gowns of black, each wearing a bow of white crepe on the left arm, walked on either side of the hearse to the Methodist church and thence to the cemetery. It was a modestly conducted funeral and gave evidence that, though ostracized from society, these unfortunates have a very tender feeling for their fellow unfortunates."

Individual families traditionally cared for the plots until the mid 1950s, when a female civic group named the Commonweal Girls requested a 1.0 mill levy for the upkeep of the Lone Tree Cemetery. When the measure passed, a cemetery board was appointed by the County Commissioners, a tool shed was built, and the grass was mowed and weeded. In 1958, a paid employee was hired, and in 1990, a lawn sprinkler system was installed. In the 1950s, burial plots were $20 for locals and $25 for non-locals. Today, plots cost $350.

These are but a few of the many interesting facts about the region. The town and the region have gone through many changes over the years, but a few constants remain. The Telluride tradition of helping one another has transcended time, philosophical and socio-economic stratification. Intensity, individuality, risk taking, and love of the outdoors are common traits and passions found in those who live in this area. The philosophical, psychological, and political battlefields are always ripe for new participants, but, generally, and over time, there is a high tolerance for diversity. Walk softly, listen, and pay attention, you will experience something special and unique.

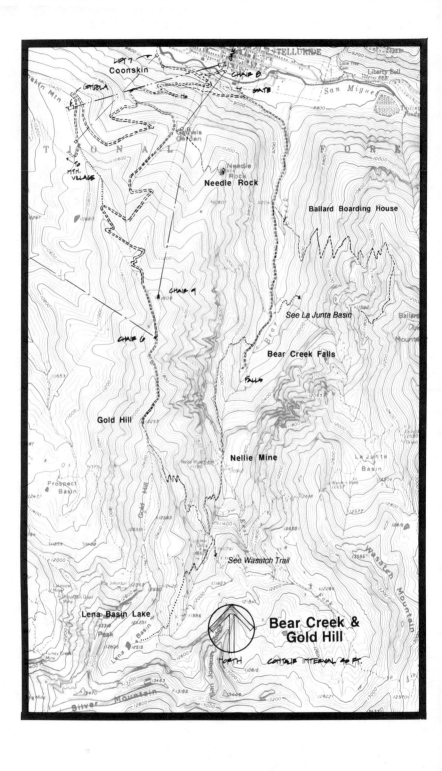

Bear Creek & Gold Hill

1 BALLARD BOARDINGHOUSE

Time:	**Plan on 6-8 hours minimum round trip**
Distance:	**Approximately seven miles round trip**
Elevation Gain:	**Approximately 3,320 feet**
Maximum Elevation:	**Approximately 12,080 feet**
Difficulty:	**Extremely difficult**
Trailhead:	**Approximately 1.1 miles from the Bear Creek bridge to the first open meadow**
Trail end:	**Same as trailhead**
Map:	**U.S.G.S. Telluride Quadrangle**

Snow often lingers in the couloirs below Ballard Mountain. This hike is extremely strenuous, so wait, get in shape and let the snow melt. I like to do this when the grass grows gold and the weather is stable. When fall's color-drama paints the landscape, the invigoration of the crisp fall air and the excitement of the rapid changes make high-country hiking a spectacular adventure. The best time to hike to the boardinghouse is in the fall when yellows and oranges appear.

This hike is only recommended for those who are altitude acclimatized and in shape and should be avoided by those who are squeamish of heights. It is advisable to do at least two other full day high altitude hikes before attempting this one.

The hike begins about a mile, twenty minutes, up Bear Creek. At the first clearing or meadow, which is a grassy opening running down to the creek on the left, look for a metal stock gate at the creek and cross where it is safe and comfortable. Meander up the slope about 200 feet to find an obvious trail which heads upstream, south, and eventually passes the remains of an old log structure. The trail continues across a 200 foot slide path and enters the aspens. Go left at the first fork and then the trail switches back through a thick, dark, evergreen forest where many downed logs restrict the trail. After many steep switchbacks, the trail swings back across the avalanche path, through a forested area. Go right at the next fork, taking the most well traveled trail.

After about two, perhaps two and a half, hours of hiking, you will see a distinctly different opening with a large spire and other rock formations, sometimes referred to as the "rock garden." Walk up the the middle of this rocky clearing, beyond the spire, to find a trail going through a weakness in the rock, heading left. The trail continues up many steep switchbacks in the trees. Look to the south for the remains of the old boardinghouse from the trail before you reach the ridge. The roof has caved in and only the rubble now remains.

You have views of Gold Hill, Wilson Peak, Lone Cone, Little Cone, Tomboy Road, and Marshall Basin; and from this ridge you can walk directly up to climb Ballard Mountain or go right, south, traversing under the peak, beyond the rocky spire, and drop down to the boardinghouse. To reach the boardinghouse, traverse above tree line on the most obvious trail in lush alpine tundra often ablaze with wildflowers in July.

An ice axe is recommended early in the hiking season when there can be snow in the gullies on this traverse. A steel cable is visible about 100 feet below the trail. After passing the cable, drop down on the left side of the rock outcroppings to below an old mine portal and an opening in the rock.

Wander down on the remains of an old rock trail which eventually crosses over a ridge and heads toward the trees below. The boardinghouse is approximately a 500 foot descent through the trees to a ledge overlooking an incredible view of Telluride. This ledge can make squeamish hikers feel dizzy.

Overlooking Bear Creek and Telluride, the remains of the boarding-house are located below the notch on Ballard Mountain approximately two thirds of the way down the broken rocky ridge at 11,502 feet, surrounded by rocky cliffs. It takes me about three and a half hours from the bridge in town to this point.

This is an exciting hike for the adventuresome, exceptionally fit, acclimatized hiker. In bad weather, the descent to the boardinghouse can be treacherous. One hiker said, "It was like a ladder in places. That's one hike I wouldn't want to repeat."

On the return, it is easy to hike too high and miss the traverse. Beware of steep scrambling and a treacherous couloir crossing if you go too high. When hiking back up from the boardinghouse, stop before the last rock going up the ridge to find the traverse trail. From the boardinghouse it can take about three hours to hike back to town. Plan on six to eight hours for this round trip from the Bear Creek bridge in town.

Once known as a good place to get a drink near Telluride, and the best whiskey in the United States during Prohibition, the Ballard boardinghouse stood proudly, nestled among the trees below Ballard Mountain.

Ballard Boardinghouse; good view of descent point to building.

After Mortimer and Tom Ballard left Iowa and arrived in Colorado in the early 1880s, they located the Golden Butterfly Lode and the Minute Placer claims on the mountain which was named after them. The location on their claims' certificates indicates that the area was precipitous, inaccessible, and exposed to snow slides.

That didn't stop Mortimer from working the lode for four years and selling one fourth of it to Charles Painter for the handsome profit of $1,000. Mortimer operated stamp mills at Mill Creek and at Bridal Veil, while Tom was the prospector who located the Ballard Lode. After Mortimer and Mary Jane's second child, Nellie, was born, they moved to a small farm below Placerville where their main garden product was onions. Nellie was later known to her family, endearingly named by her husband, as the "pearl of the onion patch."

This hike is a real jewel, but definitely only for a few, well-qualified adventure seekers.

↬

2 BEAR CREEK FALLS

Time:	**3/4 to 1 1/2 hours to the falls**
Distance:	**Approximately 2 miles to the falls**
Elevation Gain:	**1,040 feet.**
Maximum Elevation:	**9,800 feet.**
Difficulty:	**Easy**
Trailhead:	**San Miguel River crossing at Pine Street (Bear Creek bridge)**
Trail End:	**Same as Trailhead**
Map:	**U.S.G.S. Telluride Quadrangle**

Thanks to the San Miguel Land Trust, a local non-profit organization dedicated to preserving land in its natural state, along with the Town of Telluride, Bear Creek has been acquired as open space and wildlife sanctuary. The Bear Creek road has played a significant role in history. A colorful and interesting interpretive map is published by the San Miguel Land Trust. Maps can be purchased in many outlets in town. The sale proceeds go to support the non-profit land trust's important activities in the region. Use the beautifully illustrated, informative maps to accompany you on your walk.

This is one of the more popular, short hikes in Telluride. Hikes up Bear Creek road offer a wide variety of experiences. The access from town along the creek is a well-traveled jeep road, closed to motorized vehicles, but frequently used by hikers, bikers, and horses. This hike is also the gateway to many hikes in the Bear Creek Basin, including the Nellie Mine, Gold Hill, Lena Basin Lake, Ballard Mountain, La Junta Basin, and the Wasatch Trail. You may want to avoid mid-day travel in the heat of the summer, when horse flies are a horrible annoyance. This hike, a popular local run, walk, or bike from town is especially good for those with limited time.

Bear Creek was once a sacred ceremonial ground for the Ute Indians, and it is still a great place for a meditative walk. Raspberries and strawberries,

Bear Creek Falls (by Eric Davidson)

which grow wild along the road in late summer, once attracted black bears to the area. Plant life is varied and interesting throughout the hike.

Where the road bends to a degree to the right and there is a flat area on the left and large boulders on the right, you will see cement walls, just below the last steep grade, where the remnants of the foundation of the San Miguel Consolidated Mill, the biggest mill in the area was located. This was at one time owned by L.L. Nunn.

In approximately 1914, Cleona Crozier lived in Bear Creek in the old bunk and boarding house while her father disassembled the mill and her mother took in boarders. She rode horses and mules to school with her three brothers. One day they saw thirteen snow slides in the canyon. Ordinarily, they called Mom to announce their safe arrival at school, but one winter morning the phone did not ring. When their father and his workmen set out to search for the children, they found horse tracks leading to a slide. Amidst sobs, their father and the men crossed the avalanche to discover tracks on the other side leading to the four frightened children nestled safely together under a shed. These children picked wild red raspberries in the summer and slid in pans down the hillsides by the mill in winter.

When the girls working in the red light district were not allowed into Telluride on the railroad, they were sneaked in on the Bear Creek road.

The falls are beyond the big climbing boulder, approximately 1/4 mile beyond the Wasatch Trail cutoff at the end of the road. At the top, walk off the main road to the right just before the big rock and find a nice trail to the pool below Bear Creek falls.

Above and left of the falls is a couloir which is a popular spring ski route from Ophir. Avalanche hazard can be extreme. If you plan to ski, use caution. A guide is also recommended.

3 GOLD HILL

Time:	**3 1/2 to 5 hours to the top of Gold Hill**
Distance:	**Approximately 4.9 miles to the top of Gold Hill**
Elevation Gain:	**Approximately 3,560 feet**
Maximum Elevation:	**12,320 feet**
Difficulty:	**Difficult**
Trailhead:	**Bear Creek road to the Wasatch Trail cutoff**
Trail End:	**Same as trailhead**
Map:	**U.S.G.S. Telluride Quadrangle**

At the top of Gold Hill, the views are awe-inspiring. You get a feel for ski area expansion plans and a sense of the profound as you take time to enjoy the breathtaking panorama.

You can start at the top of lift #9 or come up Bear Creek and go from the Nellie Mine (see Nellie Mine hike). Soon after passing the mine, continue right at the fork and the trail climbs steeply away from the creek zigging back and forth and then swings back to the creek again. Do not cross the creek at the trail sign there; take a sharp right and walk on a well-defined, old wagon road to the top of the ski area. While walking up this road, watch for stunted and full purple Indian paintbrush and a few white columbine high on the trail.

This is a straightforward hike with spectacular 180-degree views at the top of: the La Sal Mountains, Lizard Head, the Wilsons, the town of Telluride, and Lone Cone. Other prominent features include La Junta Basin, the Ballard boardinghouse, Wasatch Mountain, La Junta Peak, Ballard Mountain, and St. Sophia Ridge.

From the top of the road to Gold Hill, it is possible to walk into Lena Basin, directly south, or to ascend Gold Hill for more lofty views. You can also stay high on the ridge and view the lake in Lena Basin from above. The views of Alta Lakes and Prospect Basin are incredible from this ridge. It takes about an hour to walk to the top of the ridge from the high point on the road. It is more direct (and strenuous) to scramble up to the ridge before the road reaches the top.

Several descents are possible from the top of the road from Gold Hill. You can walk right, to the north, down the ski area. This is a four mile descent from the top of Gold Hill into town. Probably the fastest route is about a two hour walk down See Forever to town. For a contrast of mining and ski mountain perspectives, and a view of the front of the mountain without snow, this descent is interesting. Another return is to go into Lena Basin and walk back down Bear Creek, or you can simply double back and return via the road.

For an interesting, full-day adventure, spectacular sights, and a reminder of Telluride's historical heritage, follow the echoes of the past and walk up Gold Hill. Grover Williams built the road to the top of Gold Hill around 1954 to get to his mining claims. Gold Hill was aptly named for its rich veins and was once one of the richest mining areas in the world, producing fourteen ounces of gold per ton. The gold content there was supposedly twenty times that of Ouray, and many diggings are still visible.

༃

4 LA JUNTA BASIN from Bear Creek

Time:	**6 to 8 hours from Bear Creek bridge to the Bridal Veil power plant**
Distance:	**Approximately 7.5 miles to the power plant**
Elevation Gain:	**4,000 feet**
Maximum Elevation:	**12,820 feet at the saddle crossing into Bridal Veil Basin**
Difficulty:	**Difficult to extremely difficult (There are two steep scree crossings leading into the basin which can be extremely difficult.)**
Trailhead:	**Approximately 3/4 mile up Bear Creek road in a meadow where a large, flat, dome-shaped rock lies near the creek**
Trail End:	**Power plant in Bridal Veil Basin**
Map:	**U.S.G.S. Telluride Quadrangle**

This is a strenuous hike with a formidable scree slope traverse where some have turned back. The La Junta Basin trailhead is more than a thirty minute walk up the Bear Creek road at a grassy meadow by a flat, dome-shaped rock. It is three quarters of the way up to the rock, the last level grassy area next to the road below Bear Creek Falls.

Cross the creek wherever comfortably and safely possible and work your way left of the avalanche path and the creek bed coming out of La Junta Basin where a trail zigs back and forth through a dense forest. While there may be many downed trees crossing the path, this is a good trail. It continues to the rock wall above, where the trail has been blasted to La Junta Basin. It was a feat of love and hard labor by miners to cut this part of the trail through solid rock.

You may pass parts of the tramway along the trail through the trees. On one metal tram holder, "1886 Patent" is written. Please be considerate and leave these artifacts for others to enjoy. Just before crossing the trail blasted through the rock, look below into Bear Creek for the remnants of the mill there. You will see the cement foundation.

Trailhead at Bear Creek to La Junta Basin.

Beyond the rock wall, the trail gets washed out and scary, requiring a bit of scrambling to the ruins of the Orient and the La Junta mines. (It can take approximately two hours to walk to this point.) In the summer of 1996, my son Blake found a note under a rock, left by a weary, scared hiker indicating that he had turned around to go back over the pass, the saddle above, rather than risk this traverse.

Beyond the broken down building sites in the trees, the trail continues, crossing an open scree field, heading toward the rocky spires. The trail crosses the creek bed and angles up through the brush to a flat spot where a jeep road begins.

This road goes over the saddle between Wasatch Mountain and La Junta Peak into Bridal Veil Basin where a tiny, unnamed lake, known among old timers as "Primrose Lake," sits. This is a great spot for a lunch break and an overlook into Bridal Veil Basin.

Go left and drop down off this road into Bridal Veil Basin. The road meanders through meadows and small ponds to an old cabin on the creek coming out of the lake at the saddle.

During wildflower season, usually mid-July to mid-August, this is an indescribably beautiful, breathtaking adventure in color. Hues of blue, purple, violet, pink, red, orange, and white speckle the verdant, lush landscape. You will want to record this multicolor experience on film, so bring your camera.

Stay left when you have a choice on the main road to return to the power plant. You will pass the Lewis Mine and the Blue Lake roads, which are to the right, as you drop down to lower Bridal Veil Creek.

While mining in La Junta Basin, Oscar Blixt considerately waved his lantern to signal his safe arrival to his wife Lena. She worked for the phone company in town. She rested more easily after seeing the signal that her husband was secure in the basin, ready to work. Oscar Blixt was rumored to have "salted" a mine in the basin. This means to get chunks of gold from elsewhere and place them in the mine to attract a potential buyer.

There are alluring and unconfirmed ghost story rumors at this exploration site. An old miner was reportedly seen, beckoning a working miner to continue digging.

ᗢ

─**5 LENA BASIN LAKE**─

Time:	**4 to 5 hours to the lake; take all day for this hike**
Distance:	**Approximately 4.8 miles, one way**
Elevation Gain:	**3,755 feet**
Maximum Elevation:	**12,515 feet**
Difficulty:	**Difficult**
Trailhead:	**Bear Creek road or at the top of lift #9**
Trail End:	**Same as trailhead**
Map:	**U.S.G.S. Telluride Quadrangle**

While many hike to Gold Hill, the hike to Lena Basin lake, the source of Bear Creek, is little traveled and you will no doubt find solitude in this special, serene place which is well worth the effort.

There are two routes into Lena Basin. One is from Bear Creek, the other is from the top of lift #9. From Bear Creek, the trail to Lena Basin continues from the Nellie Mine (see Nellie Mine hike). After the mine, you continue past the East Fork on the Wasatch Trail, walking on the west, right, side of the creek, up switchbacks to where it crosses Bear Creek. From here, the most direct route into Lena Basin is to continue walking up the creek on the west, right, side and to take a strenuous zig zag path through the steep grassy slope above, then to cross the creek on the left walking under San Joaquin Ridge and essentially follow the creek into the basin above. (It can take in-shape locals two and a half hours from the Bear Creek bridge to this juncture. Often the average person may take two hours from the Nellie Mine to the lake.)

Lena Basin

The trail continues below the San Joaquin Ridge and the scree slope ahead and again crosses Bear Creek. At this point, the route swings left, beyond the dark rocks. From the last creek crossing, it may take another hour to get into the basin.

In Lena Basin, two tiny clear azure lakes sit at 12,515 feet surrounded by 13,000 feet peaks. Palmyra Peak, Silver Mountain, and San Joaquin Ridge tower above these pristine ponds. It takes just about two hours from the Nellie Mine to reach the lake in Lena Basin by this route.

Another way into Lena Basin is to go from Gold Hill (see Gold Hill hike). Walk left, south, of the ridge to Gold Hill and drop down to the trail leading directly into Lena Basin. Walking along this ridge involves some scrambling, but the views are worth the work. Views of the La Sal Mountains, Lizard Head, the Wilsons, Lone Cone, the town of Telluride, Prospect Basin, Alta Lakes, Ballard Mountain, San Joaquin Ridge, Palmyra Peak, and St. Sophia Ridge are spectacular!

The Gold Hill ridge route can be used as a return from Lena Basin. (If the Gondola is running, you can walk down See Forever and ride it down.) Stay high and left as you walk out of Lena Basin. This return trail goes left across grassy slopes and eventually hits the ridge. A number of diagonal animal trails angle through the scree below Palmyra Peak. Below and to the right, the road returns to Bear Creek above the Nellie Mine.

You can also continue to the Telluride Trail and back down to town. It takes about two hours to walk down See Forever to town for this complete circle.

6 NELLIE MINE

Time:	**2 hours to the Nellie Mine**
Distance:	**Approximately 2.8 miles to the mine**
Elevation Gain:	**2,430 feet**
Maximum Elevation:	**11,190 feet**
Difficulty:	**Moderately difficult**
Trailhead:	**San Miguel River crossing at Pine Street**
Trail End:	**Same as trailhead**
Map:	**U.S.G.S. Telluride Quadrangle**

The hike up Bear Creek road to the Wasatch Trail cutoff is approximately forty minutes for an in-shape local. (To estimate your time to the mine, double the time it took you to the cutoff.) At the Wasatch Trail cutoff on the road, a level spot beside tall pine trees provides a photographic viewpoint of Bear Creek Falls. A sign designates the Wasatch Trail which heads to the right, away from Bear Creek. Follow the switchbacks through the rock gorge to the first meadow. It is approximately one mile from the Bear Creek cutoff to the Nellie Mine.

This trail becomes increasingly steep, and sturdy shoes ensure better footing. Take time to notice the flowers throughout this section of the trail. Alpine poppy, wild raspberries, fireweed, monks hood, bluebells, and columbine populate the trail as it zigs up through the trees and levels out under a cliff band. (Before the rock gorge, the trail levels and comes out of the trees and an old miner's cabin can be seen under the cliffs to the right. The route to this cabin is a scree scramble up a rocky creek bed.)

Just before the Nellie Mine, the trail passes an overlook where the creek cascades over boulders. The trail then zigs up along a rocky cliff band, where a pathway has been chiseled into the rock wall. The sturdy wooden bridge aided mule and miner travel.

The Nellie Mine is a beautiful lunch stop where mining artifacts stimulate fantasies of the olden days. Sit down on the rock in front of the mill debris for a great view which includes a spot of town. A short walk upstream provides views of the East Fork of Bear Creek and Wasatch Basin, popular ski routes from Ophir and Gold Hill. These are high avalanche areas in the winter, and skiers have been caught and killed in slides in this treacherous terrain.

From the Nellie Mine, the trail continues up to the East Fork of Bear Creek, Gold Hill, Lena Basin, the Wasatch Trail, Bridal Veil Basin and Ophir.

Nellie Mine ruins

Old timer Jim Dalpez drilled the holes in the rock and put the boards on for the bridge. Photos of this bridge in the museum show Colorado freighter Dave Wood's mules carrying the cable for the the tramway used at the mine. On July 3, 1897, 10,810 feet of tram cable, weighing 17,000 pounds was transported to the Nellie Mine by fifty two mules. The mine was once owned by Jim's uncle, Paul Nardine. A ball mill and a power line were located up there. Miners used horses to go up and down the trail. Eventually, the mine was shut down, the mill was sold, and the power line was also torn out. (Local kids got in trouble, and one even had to go to court for pushing ore cars off the cliff there after the mine was closed.)

7 WASATCH TRAIL
from Bear Creek

Time:	**Plan on 8 hours with lunch for this loop**
Distance:	**4.8 miles to the saddle at the pass; approximately 10 miles to the power plant in Bridal Veil Basin; 12 miles total**
Elevation Gain:	**4,300 feet**
Maximum Elevation:	**13,000 feet**
Difficulty:	**Difficult**
Trailhead:	**2 miles up Bear Creek road**
Trail End:	**Power plant in Bridal Veil Basin**
Map:	**U.S.G.S. Telluride Quadrangle**
Forest Service Trail:	**508 and 513**

This is a full day's hike for most people. You will be walking steadily and steeply uphill for over four hours. Take your time and savor the sights. Bring lots of water and raingear. Review the Hiking Hints and Safety section of this guide and go prepared.

Walking up Bear Creek is always a joy and it is a good stretch in preparation for the Wasatch Trail. The trail is more difficult after it leaves the Bear Creek road.

At the top of Bear Creek, before the big rock, take the trail to the right. You will walk another forty-five minutes and then pass the Nellie Mine and mill ruins. From the cutoff at the top of Bear Creek, the trail was built to haul ore from the Nellie Mine by mule train. Just below the mine, the trail was blasted into a rock wall. The bridge there was a vital link in the transportation network to Telluride. At the Nellie Mine are some interesting remnants of yesteryear, but stay off the rubble and look from the trail.

Continue walking upward and you will reach a fork. To the left is a steeper route, East Fork of Bear Creek, which eventually leads to where you are going, the Wasatch Trail. To the right is the Wasatch Trail loop where the trail switches back and forth on a steep slope overlooking the creek. Go right. In less than an hour when you have topped out above the rock outcroppings, the trail switches back to the creek again. You walk up the creek for a short distance and come to a signage, "Trail," where you cross the creek and continue toward San Joaquin Ridge.

You will travel over a grassy knoll after crossing Bear Creek. Look back at Gold Hill road and the top of lift #9. Watch for the cairns which mark the trail in this section. After going over the top of the knoll, stay left as the trail switches eastward. You will drop down and then cross the East Fork of the creek, meeting the East Fork loop which goes left and back down. Go right here and continue walking along the creek, generally staying left, through alpine meadows. The trail sometimes gets lost in the flowers in this section, but look up ahead to see where you are going, to the saddle south of Wasatch Mountain where the trail drops into Bridal Veil Basin. Wasatch Basin, which was a popular sheep grazing area for many years, is lush with wildflowers in late summer.

From the ridge it is possible to drop directly down, traversing to the left and to go into Bridal Veil Basin or to go right and end up east of Ophir. Watch for the Wasatch Trail to drop down, right, into Bridal Veil Basin. If you continue left, around the ridge ahead, this road also goes into La Junta Basin. The road was built by the Blixt brothers, who had mining claims in the area in the 1930s.

You will walk by several small ponds and come to a fork in the road. To the right leads to the Lewis Mine. Go left at the fork in Bridal Veil Basin.

It is best to wait until the snow has thawed to do this hike. It is a common occurrence to get caught in a downpour, so if you plan to do an overnight, take a tent, and keep your sleeping bag dry.

It takes a little more than two hours for the descent to the Bridal Veil power plant from the saddle. Just follow the road, staying left. (This is the same descent described in the La Junta Basin hike.)

ॐ

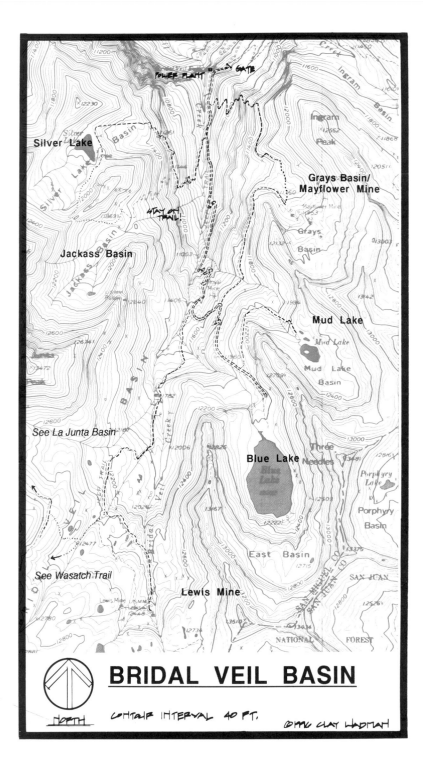

BRIDAL VEIL BASIN

CONTOUR INTERVAL 40 FT.

NORTH

© 1992 CLAY WADMAN

8 BLIXT ROAD
(Ophir to Bridal Veil Falls)

Time:	2-3 hours to reach the ridge overlooking Bridal Veil Basin; plan on 5 1/2 hours to reach the falls at the power plant
Distance:	Approximately 2.3 miles to the top of the pass; approximately 5.6 miles to the power plant
Elevation Gain:	Approximately 2,800 feet
Maximum Elevation:	13,160 feet
Difficulty:	Difficult
Trailhead:	Chapman Gulch, east of Ophir
Trail End:	Power plant, Bridal Veil Falls
Map:	U.S.G.S. Ophir Quadrangle, and Telluride Quadrangle

The old mining camp of Ophir is located about seven miles south of Telluride near the headwaters of Howard's Fork. Ophir Pass, which connects with Silverton, opened as a toll road in 1881 for wagons. The first white men came into the area over this pass. Sven Nilson was a mailman who came from Silverton. Determined to deliver children's Christmas packages, he was found frozen to death on December 23, 1888, at the top of the pass. In 1891, the railroad built two loops, commonly known as Ophir Loop, to gain elevation to go up the pass at the entrance to the valley. In 1898, five hundred people lived in Ophir. Today, 135 inhabit the town.

Driving through the town of Ophir toward Ophir Pass, you will pass the cemetery. (In 1967, a grave was dug deeper than others up to that time with the use of a backhoe. After the service, mourners left, forgetting to bury the corpse.) To reach the trailhead, continue heading east and pass two roads on your left. Stop at the third, to find the trailhead to the Blixt Road.

The walk begins in the trees opposite Swamp Canyon. In approximately half an hour of steep walking, you will overlook old building ruins and stone pillars at an old mill site. (Notice the drill holes on the opposite side of the canyon there.) This is a beautiful walk among the silver tipped trees, and the view across into Swamp Canyon is gorgeous. Soon you will come to a Y. Take the right, east, fork and pass through the gate. From there a sign reads "to Telluride is a mixture of private and public land. The mine owners haven't fenced you out. Respect their rights and property. U.S. Forest Service, tread lightly."

Bridal Veil Basin pond below Blixt Road.

The road gains elevation quickly and is a great aerobic work out. Imagine the miners coming down, sitting on the hood of their vehicles to keep the front wheels on the road as they came back to Ophir. Look across the Ophir Pass road to above Swamp Canyon to see South Lookout Peak and U.S. Grant Peak. Above tree line the road takes a big switch back in the talus and views of Ophir are spectacular. Walking on the boulders can be difficult, so watch your footing and be careful. You can reach the top in less than two hours if you walk steadily. Look east to see Crystal Lake at the top of Ophir Pass and beaver ponds below in the Ophir valley.

Heading down to Telluride, you have three choices. You can take the first saddle to your left and walk down the Wasatch Trail into Bear Creek. You may also go into La Junta Basin by continuing straight ahead on the road traversing under Wasatch Mountain. Or you can also walk straight ahead until a trail cuts down to the right and eventually connects with the road that goes through Bridal Veil Basin. It is about a two and a half hour walk to go to the power plant at Bridal Veil Falls.

9 BLUE LAKE

Time:	**4 hours round trip**
Distance:	**Approximately 5 1/4 miles round trip**
Elevation Gain:	**Approximately 2,000 feet**
Maximum Elevation:	**12,202 feet**
Difficulty:	**Moderate**
Trailhead:	**Bridal Veil power plant**
Trail End:	**Same as trailhead**
Map:	**U.S.G.S. Telluride Quadrangle**

The hike to Blue Lake begins at the power plant at Bridal Veil Falls. At a steady pace for someone acclimatized and in shape, walking to the lake should take about an hour and a half. When the flowers are in full bloom, mountain manzanita, Indian paintbrush, monks hood, elephant ears, and columbine adorn the meadows and creeks. This is a spectacular wildflower walk which ends above tree line.

Stay on the road and pass a tin roofed shed where the road switches upward, sharply to the left, away from the creek. Blue Lake is an hour from this shed. Continue walking on this main road which climbs beyond the Royal Mine ruins where you will eventually come to a Y. Take the left, toward the pointed pyramid shaped mountain in the skyline. (Blue Lake is in the basin below, to the left, east.)

Continue walking up a rocky road beside a sometimes wet, dark rock wall to another Y. (Below, in the grassy meadow to the left are the remains of a log cabin. Here the road to the left follows a pipeline to Mud Lake and Gray's Basin. See hikes. On the return, this spot is twenty minutes down from Mud Lake.) Go right, toward the three-needled pyramid shaped peak ahead. Pass a collapsed wooden bridge over a creek bed and see electric lines on wooden posts below the triangular shaped peak ahead. Continue climbing past the old wooden tram towers and beyond the wooden shed at the top of the old Polaski Tram. This tram was operated on an as needed basis.

Where the trail levels out, there are two well-preserved cabins, a bunkhouse and a coal shed. These are in use today. Stay on the road and respect this private property. Blue Lake itself is private property. It is the domestic water supply for the upper San Miguel Valley. At the lake, an old cabin is situated below the steep pinnacled ridge to the east where the main mine shaft was located, but PLEASE, stay out, for safety reasons. Test holes and tailings are seen around this azure meditative site.

I have seen bear tracks in snow patches around the lake early in the summer.

Be sure to bring extra clothes for wind protection. Winds gust wild and free in this starkly beautiful basin where rusted pipe and other debris are strewn about the lake.

Water was transported to the hydroelectric plant in the old days when there was a big barge on the lake, loaded with electric motors from which the water was pumped. The barge often leaked or sank. Mining was done only during the three months in the summer there, and ore was transported across the lake by rowboat. In the mid 1930s, a tunnel was built under the lake to cover a valve house used to regulate the pressure to transport water. The tunnel was also used like a refrigerator. A side of beef or ham was hung there for fresh-keeping, and potatoes could be kept for two to three years.

This lake was once a good fishing spot. It was stocked when miners used to walk the ridge from Blue Lake to Columbine Lake to fish. The mine had a bad experience up there one time when someone carried a boat to fish at Blue Lake. The boat sank and was stuck on top of the tunnel. The lake had to be drained to remove the boat, and, from then on, boats were forbidden on the lake.

Avalanches were so bad that the caretaker had to stay at the lake from November to June. Lonely men often went stir-crazy. One was noted to have gone insane. The telephone line was up and he sounded desperate as he spoke with miners in town. They realized he needed help and sent a party with a toboggan and snowshoes to rescue him. When the rescue team arrived at the Polaski tram, they found the caretaker had removed the ore buckets from the tram, which meant that the men had to walk up. They arrived exhausted and cold at the bunkhouse to find him gone! Needing to return to town that day they walked back down in a storm. The rescuers barely found their way down and arrived back at the Pandora Mill to find an emergency work situation.

Al Norris, one of the men who went on the rescue, had to stay up all night to work at the mill. There was no such thing as overtime in those days. The men worked when needed; it was all a part of the job.

10 BRIDAL VEIL FALLS/ POWER PLANT

Time:	3/4 hour from Pandora Mill to the bottom of the falls, add 15 to 20 minutes to reach the power plant at the top of the falls
Distance:	Approximately 1.8 miles from the Pandora Mill to the gate at the top of the falls
Elevation Gain:	Approximately 1,200 feet
Maximum Elevation:	10,000 feet
Difficulty:	Easy
Trailhead:	Pandora Mill, east of Telluride
Trail End:	Same as trailhead
Map:	U.S.G.S. Telluride Quadrangle

At the east end of the Telluride valley, Bridal Veil Falls, where the hydroelectric station stands, is the longest waterfall drop in Colorado. It is best to drive to the parking area beyond Pandora Mill to start this walk, because parking at the top of the falls is very limited. This relatively easy walk offers a spectacular westerly view of the town of Telluride and the surrounding mountain ranges.

Walk from the mill to the bottom of the falls on a moderate jeep road. During the dry weeks of summer and fall, this can be a dusty walk when jeep traffic is continuous on this road.

From 1974, when the falls were first climbed, until December, 1996, tenacious ice climbers had risked arrest to experience the surreal quiet of hanging from the steep, often mystical and grotesque cauliflower and mushroom formations of the fully frozen falls. Through the cooperative efforts of Eric Jacobson, owner of the power plant atop the falls, the Town of Telluride, and the Access Fund, a one year legal easement has been created to allow access to these falls. The rules are available around town at sporting goods shops. Essentially, they include the following: no permanent anchors may be placed in the falls; no top rope climbing allowed; no climbers under 16 years old; climbers under 18 must have written permission from a parent or guardian; climbers are prohibited from crossing or entering the property at the top of the falls.

Look, but don't risk the extreme avalanche hazard of hiking to the base of the falls in the winter. Finnboy Slides (so named after the young Finns who braved the threat of avalanche to walk to work at the Black Bear Mine above) can roar ferociously from the west side of Ingram Peak onto the road below.

Summer jeep traffic beyond the mill to the hydroelectric power plant goes both ways, but above the entrance to the plant on Black Bear Road, only one way traffic from Silverton is allowed. No motorized vehicles are allowed in Bridal Veil Basin beyond the gate. Some lovely picnic spots are available just up the road from the plant, so keep going another ten minutes before stopping to rest.

Early reports indicate that the falls were named because of their resemblance to a bride's veil. This speculation is verified in late 1800s references to the falls. Other reports suggest that the Bridal Veil Falls were named later, after a wedding couple who stood on the walkway outside the power plant above the falls. Ready to consecrate the vows of matrimony, the groom lifted his beloved bride's veil to kiss her, and she tripped and fell to her death. He stood there, stunned, tragically holding the only visible symbol of their love, the bridal veil.

The hydroelectric generating plant was built in 1907 to supply power to the Smuggler Union Mine. The plant ceased operation in 1953. It is presently privately owned and being restored. The power generated will augment the current supply. Water is piped from Blue Lake to the generator in the

Bridal Veil Falls and power plant

basement of the plant. Don't attempt to visit the power plant unless you have permission; this is private property.

The power plant was supplied with water by the surrounding lakes: Lewis Lake, Blue Lake, Mud Lake, and Silver Lake. In addition to the old trails, pipelines provide pathways to these lakes.

Bulkley Wells, the handsome Harvard graduate and manager of the Smuggler Union for over twenty years, was responsible for the romantic allure of the building. Bulkley's biographical notes reveal the drama of a gambler and a womanizer. He had the New England Exploration Company build him an apartment atop the hydro plant, which was modeled after a Swiss chalet and was supposedly used to entertain his lady friends.

An aerial tramway ran from below to transport supplies and people to the plant. Those brave souls who rode the tram found themselves standing on a four by eight foot wooden platform held by cables. It was a scary ride with just one long span of wire from top to bottom. As you walk the road, imagine the spectacular tram ride.

11 GRAY'S BASIN / MAYFLOWER MINE

Time:	1 1/2 hours to the Mayflower Mine; 3 hours round trip
Distance:	Approximately 1.6 miles to the Mayflower Mine
Elevation Gain:	Approximately 1,833 feet
Maximum Elevation:	11,953 feet
Difficulty:	Moderately difficult
Trailhead:	Approximately 100 yards beyond the power plant on the Bridal Veil Basin road, or continue up the road to a point above the Royal Mine
Trail End:	Power plant
Map:	U.S.G.S. Telluride Quadrangle

Gray's Basin, where the Mayflower Mine was located, is directly to the right of Ingram's grassy peak as you look from Telluride. This is a beautiful hike and a little traveled area off the beaten path. For mountain solitude, a beautiful basin retreat, a challenging trail finding experience, and incredible views across the canyon, this is a memorable hike.

This walk is moderate, but at times the trail disappears. A high level of route finding skill is required for this hike. Do not attempt this hike if you are ill-prepared for route finding challenges.

The trail to Gray's Basin begins at the power plant about 100 yards, approximately five minutes, up the road beyond the power plant, directly across from grassy ledges above Bridal Veil Creek, before the turfy terraces on the right give way to a rock face. Avalanche debris, fallen trees, and one single standing pine tree on the ledges across the creek mark the trailhead. (As you hike up and look to the other side of Bridal Veil Creek, use these grassy terraces as a good reference point for staying on the trail also.)

It is a challenge to find this trailhead leading to a wonderful, well hidden path into the basin. Immediately before the Bridal Veil Creek road bends left, stop, just as you see the triangular-shaped peak to the south and walk back about twenty feet and then step up above the road, another ten feet directly east to find the narrow trail.

The trail heads up beneath a prominent scree field below the rocky cliffs, eventually swinging to the right side of the scree field. You will eventually be walking below a rocky cliff band directly across from the creek coming out of Silver Lake. After walking about an hour from the start of the hike, cross a pipeline and follow it south through an open grassy area. (If you look up, you will see a tram tower at this point.) Stop before the pipeline goes up a rock band ahead and go left on a faint trail that bends right above the grassland under cliffs to a wooden power pole. Just after the power pole, go left up a rocky creek bed and climb out at a flat spot beside a pond. Going from either side of the pond, you will walk into the basin on old game trails. It is about an hour and a half to this point from the power plant. You can return via this same route, but pay close attention, as it is easy to get disoriented.

Cabin en route to Gray's Basin below Mud Lake

Instead of walking back on the same trail, you can make a loop. To do this, walk left, south, out of the basin, heading toward a standing dead tree above, cutting across the ridge. Stay fairly high and follow a faded, sometimes tricky animal trail. You will be high above the pipeline. In about 25 minutes, you will be at the cabin below Mud Lake. It is a short southern traverse from this cabin to the road where you go to the right, back down to the power plant.

Beware of walking around ruins of the Mayflower Mine because there is a 150 foot tunnel. Innocuous-looking boards or dirt may cover a death-trap, so observe from a safe distance and stay on the trails.

The cabin that you pass on the loop below Mud Lake was once a welcome retreat in a storm, stocked with emergency provisions: tea, coffee, and oatmeal left in a wooden box, covered with stove pipe to keep the animals out. Weary travelers were expected to replace goods used on their next trip by the cabin. Carved on a wood sign was a notice: "If you are ever near here at lunchtime or night, help yourself. You are heartily welcome. Remember, only a heel will violate the code of the mountains. If you do, well, don't ever let me catch you bending over."

Unconfirmed rumors of fraud were associated with the Mayflower Mine. Worthless stock in the mine was sold in England, and, supposedly, the tram ran for only one day. This was considered a highly unsuccessful mining operation, and the small tailings pile indicates there may not have been much activity here.

Building the tramway into Gray's Basin was an incredible feat. The tram took a tremendous span from the Mayflower Mine to below the tailings across from the Lone Tree Cemetery. It was a perfectly straight tramway. Leishen, a German company based in the U.S. in St. Louis and Denver, built the tram and was very proud of its accomplishment. Buckets were loaded from the upper end with slide rock, and the weight brought up the load from below. From the top down, you can still see the cut made by the tramway. Considering the distance the tramway dropped and the ruggedness of the country it spanned, this was a monumental task.

ᴣ͡ꙮ

——12 JACKASS BASIN——

Time:	**1 1/2 hours to Jackass Basin, one way**
Distance:	**Approximately 1.5 miles to the cabin at the head of Jackass Basin**
Elevation Gain:	**1,680 feet**
Maximum Elevation:	**12,200 feet**
Difficulty:	**Difficult**
Trailhead:	**Bridal Veil Creek crossing beyond the power plant**
Trail End:	**Same as trailhead**
Map:	**U.S.G.S. Telluride Quadrangle**

Take a break from the rest of the world and get into Jackass Basin. You can go on retreat in this private, barren-landscaped basin.

The hike begins at the Bridal Veil Creek crossing for the Silver Lake trail. The trail to Jackass Basin cuts left, south, at the fork, away from the Silver Lake trail, and heads toward the pyramid shaped peak at the end of the basin. A faint animal trail zigs its way on loose gravel on the right side of the creek coming out of the basin. You may discover the origin of the term "bushwhacking" as you whack your way through dense bushes up the draw and around some major boulders.

The trail is at times very faint and loose rocks mark the path into the basin. Notice the marsh marigold and the false hellebore as you climb. It can take an in-shape, acclimatized person about an hour from the creek crossing

Cabin at Jackass Basin

to the cabin at the entrance to Jackass Basin. This cabin, which sits near the creek, is a nice picnic stop. Miner brothers, Oscar and Gator Blixt, used the cabin but found little ore in the basin. There was once a ball mill in Jackass Basin which one miner carried away by mule to Ophir.

If you want to do this hike, plan to make the loop with Silver Lake and see each of the strikingly contrasting basins. To walk into Silver Lake Basin from Jackass Basin, stay right beyond the cabin where the trail levels out and climb the ridge on a footpath which cuts diagonally to a notch between the rocks. This is another great stop which affords excellent views into each basin.

It is an easy drop on a pebbled scree field down to Silver Lake, and the trail is wide enough to ride a horse. Take a lunch and make a day of this hike, or take a tent and spend the night. You will enjoy it!

13 LA JUNTA BASIN from Bridal Veil

Time:	**2 1/2 to 3 hours to the saddle between Wasatch Basin and La Junta Peak; 6-8 hours for the loop**
Distance:	**Approximately 7.5 miles from the gate at the road by the power plant to the Bear Creek bridge**
Elevation Gain:	**2,620 feet**
Maximum Elevation:	**12,820 feet**
Difficulty:	**Difficult-extremely difficult (There are two steep scree crossings below the La Junta Basin and Orient mines. This is NOT a hike for beginners.)**
Trailhead:	**Bridal Veil power plant**
Trail End:	**Bear Creek at the San Miguel River crossing**
Map:	**U.S.G.S. Telluride Quadrangle**

In July and August, the hike to La Junta Basin from the Bridal Veil power plant is a beautiful walk along Bridal Veil Creek. A multitude of wild flowers surround pristine ponds on this moderate uphill walk through grassy meadows ablaze with alpine color.

You will want to record this multi-color experience on film, so bring your camera.

This hike is on the same road that forks to the Lewis Mine and to

Wasatch Basin. Take the right fork toward Wasatch Mountain, staying right, and going north below the peak. (See Wasatch Trail hike.) At the last bench, go right.

A tiny, formally unnamed lake, called "Primrose Lake" by old timers, sits between Wasatch Mountain and La Junta Peak, just below the saddle into La Junta Basin. At 12,815 feet this beautiful lunch spot offers incredible views and a wonderful rest stop. (It is also possible to reach this little lake by going directly up the creek which flows out of the lake following the pipeline from the west at the old wooden shed by the creek in Bridal Veil Basin. This route involves some scrambling and bushwhacking, and is more strenuous than continuing on the jeep road.)

After crossing the saddle into La Junta Basin, stay to the right on the road that winds down through the canyon to the right of the creek. This is a beautiful walk, with much evidence of mining activity throughout the descent.

At a flat spot in the basin, where you will see evidence of recent mining exploration, cross the creek and drop down through the thick brush on a somewhat obscure trail that heads toward the spires below. The trail to Bear Creek cuts to the right of the spires and crosses a scree field leading to some broken-down building sites in the trees below.

From here, the trail crosses steep scree, overlooking a steep rocky gully. In a few places, the trail is washed out and requires a bit of scary scrambling; this part of the hike is a little frightening. The route continues on a narrowly chiseled path along a cliff band overlooking Bear Creek. It was a feat of love and hard labor by miners to cut this trail out of solid rock.

Look below into Bear Creek for remnants of the mill. You can see the cement foundation. The trail continues north into the trees, taking many steep, narrow switchbacks to Bear Creek below. Many fallen down trees cross the trail here. You will pass parts of the tramway along the trail through the trees. On one metal tram holder, "1886 Patent" is written. At the

La Junta Basin overlooking the Orient Mine

bottom, cross the drainage coming out of La Junta Basin and drop down to find a good spot for crossing Bear Creek.

This exit along Bear Creek is marked by a flat rock and a meadow where a small trail leads from the creek to the road. (See Bear Creek trailhead photo.) Reaching this point from the power plant takes locals approximately five hours. It is another forty-five minutes to the bridge at the bottom in town. Be aware in your descent that Bear Creek has been acquired by the Town of Telluride and the San Miguel Land Trust as a wildlife sanctuary dedicated to open space.

Plan on at least six hours, and perhaps eight, for this hike from the power plant to town via La Junta Basin and Bear Creek. Be sure to take appropriate clothing and gear, including a flashlight and matches. Many have been lost in this little traveled basin, and it is wise to be prepared.

Remember, if you see miners exploring in this area, you are the trespasser. Treat them with consideration and respect; some of these good Samaritans have been known to save lives, offering food and shelter to lost or disoriented hikers after sunset.

The Blixt Road was cut by three Swedish brothers who worked mining claims in La Junta Basin. It connects to Chapman Gulch east of Ophir, and goes under Wasatch Mountain. Hair-raising stories have been told about jeeps on the narrow, steep switch backed Blixt road. Miners sat on the hoods to ease the vehicles down steep sections, and jeeps were hooked together and pulled over the top by a bulldozer.

Ghosts have been reported to inhabit La Junta Basin. One miner dreamed of wandering through old ruins when a cold sensation chilled him from his side. He sensed a much older miner trying to communicate. "Keep drilling," the old man said. Another old miner was reportedly seen beckoning a working miner to continue digging.

The enterprising Blixt brothers were the first to take an air compressor into La Junta Basin. It was in La Junta Basin where Oscar Blixt considerately waved his lantern to signal his safe arrival to his wife Lena, who was working for the phone company in town. She rested more easily after seeing the signal that her husband was secure in the basin, ready to work.

Oscar Blixt was once said to have "salted" a mine in the basin, meaning he got chunks of gold from elsewhere and placed them in the mine to attract a potential buyer.

〜

14 LEWIS MINE

Time:	**Plan on 2 1/2 hours to reach the Lewis Mine from the power plant at Bridal Veil Falls.**
Distance:	**3.4 miles to the mine**
Elevation Gain:	**2,328 feet**
Maximum Elevation:	**12,448 feet at the mine (12,700 feet at Lewis Lake; 13,058 at the ridge crossing to Columbine Lake)**
Difficulty:	**Moderately difficult**
Trailhead:	**Bridal Veil Falls power plant**
Trail End:	**Same as trailhead**
Map:	**U.S.G.S. Telluride Quadrangle**

The hike to the Lewis Mine is a kaleidoscopic adventure most years between mid-July and mid-August when the prismatic procession of knee deep wildflowers is spectacular. There is lush vegetation aside Bridal Veil Creek's small pools and boulder filled drops, as unnamed streams flush into the creek, moistening and mystifying this enchanting basin.

Stay on the road, pass the Royal Mine, and continue right at the Y below the pyramid shaped unnamed peak where several finger-like spires project from the ridge. (There is speculation that these were supposed to be named Three Needles and that the summit now known as such was mistakenly identified.)

The basin levels out where a small shack sits beside a low water pond. Cross the creek and veer right of the gully, avoiding the dead end at the small basin here. Stay on the road that goes left of the pipeline ahead and wind upward past two small ponds in an open meadow. The road rises another two hundred feet. The Blixt Road to Ophir is visible on the right at the end of the basin. On the left in the distance you will see a diagonal road which goes over the ridge to Columbine Lake. Steer toward that road on the left, which leads from Lewis Lake to the ridge. Eventually, the road drops and there is a fork. Take the left fork which swings around two more small ponds and back up Bridal Veil Creek to the Lewis Mine.

You can't see the Lewis Mill until you're 100 yards below it. After nearly two and a half hours of walking, it is a nice surprise. This is one of the better preserved sites in the area, but the roof is disintegrating and the building may soon collapse.

The Lewis Mill was state of the art, using a water flotation wheel during its day, which only lasted from 1912 to November of 1913. Bringing up the machinery used here was an arduous task, made easier by the Blixt brothers' road improvements. Beyond the mill is the mine superintendent's cabin on the right. Today, this testimonial to an era gone by is rumored to be inhabited by friendly ghosts. Some reliable sources have seen a woman wearing a scarf, carrying a metal bucket, walking on moonlit nights from the cabin to the creek and back.

A trail starts in the scree beyond the cabin on the right and cuts back left crossing the creek just below Lewis Lake. To continue beyond Lewis Mine, it

Bridal Veil Basin from above Lewis Mine

is another hour's walk through loose rock and avalanche paths to the ridge where you look directly across the basin to Columbine Lake. (Plan on eight hours round trip from the power plant to this ridge and back.)

The hike beyond the Lewis Mine is not for low top shoes; so be sure you have sturdy footwear. To get to Ophir Pass from Columbine Lake, you can either continue on the road to the left, which takes you down and around, or you can stay right, crossing the meadow on the far right side of the lake. You probably have less chance of getting lost if you stay on the road here.

The more difficult and challenging way is to head toward a grassy knoll left of the lake which goes over a saddle to a formally no-name lake, known as "Ruby Lake" among old timers. On the saddle it is necessary to scramble and to climb down a snow couloir to the trail which is right of "Ruby Lake". For this route, it would be helpful to have a rope. There are several foot trails which lead to a jeep road on the left. After approximately forty-five minutes, you will pass a working mine and eventually connect with the Ophir Pass Road. This route involves ingenuity and good decision making skills. I recommend returning back to the power plant, but if you go to Ophir Pass, be sure to have a ride from there or plan to camp.

15 MUD LAKE

Time:	**Plan on 1 1/2 hours to cross the creek below the pipeline leading into Mud Lake; nearly 2 hours to Mud Lake itself**
Distance:	**It is approximately 3.3 miles from the power plant to Mud Lake.**
Elevation Gain:	**2,120 feet**
Maximum Elevation:	**12,240 feet**
Difficulty:	**Moderately difficult**
Trailhead:	**Bridal Veil power plant**
Trail End:	**Same as trailhead**
Map:	**U.S.G.S. Telluride Quadrangle**

Mud Lake is a man-made water storage reservoir for the power plant. It is on the pipeline from Blue Lake. It is a welcome retreat from the high country hubbub, a place where you will find solitude. Above tree line, this marshy, pristine valley is alive with beautiful alpine flowers.

Take the road above the power plant which goes to Blue Lake. Keep walking past a small wooden shack on the right below a cascading falls. Continue left up a steep, loose, stone switchback that passes a steel gate attached to the dark rock wall on the right. At the top of this switchback is a Y. The road to the right goes to Blue Lake. The left leads to Mud Lake.

This road leads to a cabin site on the creek coming out of Mud Lake Basin. See Gray's Basin photo. At this cabin was a sign on a box of "survival staples" which read: "If you are ever near here at lunch time or night, help yourself, you are heartily welcome. Remember only a heel will violate the code of the mountains. If you do, well, don't ever let me catch you bending over."

To get into Mud Lake Basin from this cabin, walk up left, north of the creek, between boulders across the grassy benches to the meadows above. Stay left of the gorge and find faint animal trails or bushwhack above to below the rock band, left of the falls. You will see the pipeline across the basin to your right as you ascend toward the falls. The trail is more distinct toward the end, left of the steep stream bed. To the left beyond the falls in the meadow above is a tiny pond, a tarn, before Mud Lake.

You can return by the same route or follow the pipeline as it swings to your left, south, to the road below Blue Lake. You can also go back down to the cabin below and follow the pipeline for a short distance and when it begins to descend more steeply, go higher to your right, north, and find an animal trail which leads into Gray's Basin. (See Gray's Basin hike to find return directions.)

This is a neat hike and can be done in three hours from the power plant and back.

Pipeline to Mud Lake

16 SILVER LAKE

Time:	**1 1/2 to 2 hours to Silver Lake**
Distance:	**Approximately 1.6 miles from the power plant to Silver Lake**
Elevation Gain:	**1,668 feet from the power plant**
Maximum Elevation:	**11,788 feet**
Difficulty:	**Difficult, a few short stretches of extreme**
Trailhead:	**Bridal Veil Creek crossing, above the power plant**
Trail End:	**Same as trailhead**
Map:	**U.S.G.S. Telluride Quadrangle**

Silver Lake is one of the more beautiful spots in the spectacular San Juans. This is a good hike to take after you have acclimatized. The hike is aerobic, one of the steepest, but take your time, drink lots of water, and go. You won't regret your sweat.

Walk approximately ten minutes beyond the power plant to the creek crossing for Silver Lake. There is a large rock on the right, or down creek, on which you can carefully step across the creek. Or try taking off your shoes, rolling up your pants, and freezing your feet for a quick dash across. This initial creek crossing can be challenging in high water.

The trail swings left immediately after crossing the creek. You will come to a fork where you cut to the right. The left trail continues toward the stream coming out of Jackass Basin. Go right to Silver Lake and walk up in thick brush on loose gravel as the climb steepens.

This trail becomes steeper and more strenuous, so go slowly and drink lots of water. Take the time to enjoy the views as you hike up and look across Bridal Veil Canyon into Gray's Basin where an old boardinghouse still stands.

After hiking up nearly 1,000 feet, you will cross a meadow and see the water coming out of the lake. To the right of the water is the tunnel which goes under the lake. Climb another 100 feet to the lake. This pristine alpine lake sits at 11,788 feet.

Take a picnic with you to enjoy the views at the lake, and stretch this into a relaxing day's excursion. The hiking time round trip from the power plant to Silver Lake can be less than four hours, which even includes time to relax and explore the area a little.

To make a loop into Jackass Basin, walk back to the left of Silver Lake through the marshes to the jagged pinnacles. Look for the saddle in the rocky ridge where the big boulder is sitting on its side. Drop left into Jackass Basin

Falls into Silver Lake

and continue left on an animal trail that fades in and out.

The trail from Jackass Basin back down to Bridal Veil Creek is faint and hard to follow at times, but stay left of the creek coming out of the basin and you will find the route that ends this enchanting loop back at the Bridal Veil Creek crossing.

Silver Lake was used like a pasturing area for injured miners unable to continue the hard strain of work underground. They tended mules and horses there until they were able to return to work in the mines. Silver Lake was also used as a watershed for the power plant. The tunnel under the lake was used to transport the water down.

Fishing at Silver Lake has been excellent, so bring your rod. You will see huge trout but they are a challenge to catch. In the summer of 1991, my son Scott caught a 22-inch trout, large enough to feed two families. His bait is still a well guarded secret. Ed Baker, Dale Dyer, and Billy Mahoney Sr. put the original fish in this lake. Those fingerlings grew to fourteen inches in the first year. It wasn't uncommon to catch 100 fish in the old days and fishermen used old "rain barrels" to help keep the fish fresh until they were ready to eat.

17 WASATCH TRAIL
from Bridal Veil

Time:	**2 1/2 to 3 hours to the saddle crossing into Bear Creek, about 6-8 hours to complete the loop to town**
Distance:	**Approximately 12 miles**
Elevation Gain:	**2,700 feet**
Maximum Elevation:	**13,050 feet**
Difficulty:	**Difficult**
Trailhead:	**Bridal Veil power plant**
Trail End:	**Bear Creek at the San Miguel River crossing**
Map:	**U.S.G.S. Telluride Quadrangle**
Forest Service Trail:	**#508**

Bridal Veil Basin to Bear Creek is one of the more beautiful hikes around Telluride. Wasatch Basin was once a popular sheep grazing area and is often ablaze with wild color. Water is abundant here, but do not drink it. Walking up Bridal Veil Basin from the power plant is a romantic adventure. Cascading falls meander and plunge through sometimes waist-deep wildflowers flourishing aside the crystal creek as pristine pools and remnants of mining history stir the imagination.

Beyond the power plant, the jeep road continues above the creek, passing an old tin-roof shack on the right, below the Royal Mine. The road rapidly gains elevation as it switches to the left.

When it swings back right, along the creek, you will find a fork. Do not take the more established trail to the left which leads to Blue Lake, Mud Lake, and Gray's Basin. Stay to the right and walk along the creek on a beautiful stone walkway. Steel bars, which once held cable, stick out in the rock below.

A critical juncture lies ahead after you pass the old Blixt brothers' cabin site in the flats. At the cabin site in the flats, cross the creek by the pipeline and continue on the road leading to the right. It may take about one and a half hours to this point from the power plant.

While it is tempting to cut across the meadows, stay on the road because many potential off road hazards exist. The road winds up and around the small ponds, sometimes referred to as tarns. After passing at least three of these tarns, the road swings left, dropping into a flat spot,

Saddle to Wasatch Trail from Bridal Veil Basin

where it forks. The left fork leads to the Lewis Mine and the right leads to Bear Creek and the Wasatch Trail. Be sure to go back far enough in the basin to cross into Bear Creek on the Wasatch Trail. Look to the end of the basin to see the scree, gravel-like, side of the ridge. You will go over the saddle there. When you have reached a high bench, there is a traverse which goes both left and right. Go left to the next saddle crossing. A sign and a cairn on the saddle to the right indicate the descent to Bear Creek.

Cross over the saddle and descend into a beautiful, water-filled meadow, where the stream bed flows in several directions. At the end of the meadow, the trail continues to the right of the stream. Next, it winds across the ridge on the right-hand side of the draw. Then the trail heads down, crossing the stream, winding over a knoll to Bear Creek. (To the right here is the East Fork of Bear Creek. That route is less traveled and steeper. I prefer crossing the creek and going over the knoll ahead.) The trail drops down off the knoll and crosses the creek, meeting the Gold Hill road. Veer right on a small trail which starts next to the creek and then swings left away from the creek and down to the Nellie Mine. Just below the mine, the trail was blasted into the side of a rock wall. The bridge here was a vital link in the transportation network of the area.

It is best to do this hike when the snow and ice have thawed. After the bridge, the trail continues down in a series of steep switchbacks to the Bear Creek road. From there, it is a leisurely forty-five minute stroll to the Bear Creek bridge in town. Often this seems much longer, so stop and rest a minute. Look up at Bear Creek Falls, and stretch. The walk down is beautiful, and a few minutes' relaxation will help you to enjoy it.

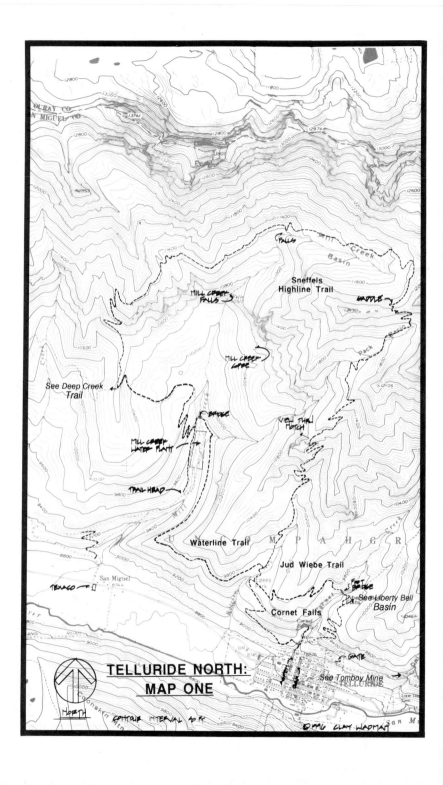

OURAY CO
SAN MIGUEL CO

Mill Creek Basin

FALLS

Sneffels
Highline Trail

SADDLE

MILL CREEK
FALLS

MILL CREEK
GATE

See Deep Creek
Trail

BRIDGE

VIEW THRU
NOTCH

MILL CREEK
WATER PLANT

TRAIL HEAD

Waterline Trail

Jud Wiebe Trail

TEXACO

San Miguel

FOOT
BRIDGE
See Liberty Bell
Basin

Cornet Falls

GATE

TELLURIDE NORTH:
MAP ONE

NORTH

CONTOUR INTERVAL 40 FT.

See Tomboy Mine

TELLURIDE

© 1996 CLAY WADMAN

18 ALDER CREEK

Time:	**Plan on 5 hours round trip on the Alder Creek trail**
Distance:	**5.5 miles one way**
Elevation Gain:	**Approximately 600 feet up and down**
Maximum Elevation:	**10,600 feet**
Difficulty:	**Moderate**
Trailhead:	**10,665 feet at the top of Last Dollar Road #638**
Trail End:	**(Junction with the Dallas trail on the Ouray district of the Uncompahgre National Forest)**
Map:	**U.S.G.S. Sams Quadrangle; Trails Illustrated Topo Silverton, Ouray, Telluride, Lake City**
Forest Service Trail:	**#510**

Alder Creek trail which stretches north to south across Hastings Mesa, was originally a stock driveway. This a little different walk than most in the area, in that you don't get the views like many other trails. Mostly sheep men and cattlemen used the trail. It doesn't get a lot of use and is a nice, quiet walk in the trees most of the way.

Start at the top of Last Dollar Road. Go approximately one fourth of a mile beyond the Whipple Mountain trailhead to the top of the road. 4 wheel drive is recommended on this road. A few campsites and a bulletin board mark the trailhead. Look at the map on the bulletin board and start walking north. This primarily flat trail heads downward and then contours through a dense forest with deadfall toward Hayden and North Pole peaks. The trail continues into upper Alder Creek and climbs up to a creek crossing at a small meadow where the remains of an old cabin stand under Hayden Peak. In July of 1996, volunteers from the Sierra Club camped here to clear the avalanche debris from the trail. The painstaking work of removing gigantic fallen logs was done by hand, with no mechanized tools, under the direction of Bill Dunkelberger. The path continues to traverse and climbs to an intermittent waterfall and crosses a slide path.

After contouring out to the end of the ridge line, the trail drops down into a mixed conifer and aspen forest. As it passes a few open aspen meadows, notice the interesting variety of tree carvings. Soon the trail drops down to the trail junction with the Dallas trail near the wilderness boundary. To this point from the trailhead on Last Dollar Road, it may take approximately two and one half hours.

Alder Creek

Walk back to the trailhead on Last Dollar Road at this time, as the connections at the end of the Dallas trail are confusing and it's easy to get lost. You are secluded in the trees and it is hard to see the landmarks around. I spent nearly four hours searching for the take off from the Dallas trail to the West Dallas Creek road and I am still unclear about the linkage at the end there. It is poorly marked and there are many other trails intersecting the Dallas trail. The Forest Service hopes to close the area to vehicles and to mark the trail more clearly in the future.

Hastings Mesa was named for George Hastings, who hauled cattle from Denver in the late 1870s. George drove the wagon and his wife led the horses and cattle. After a three month trek over the Continental Divide, they decided not to attempt to get over Dallas Divide and spent the winter with the Ute Indians in Montrose. When Louis Grosso arrived on Hastings Mesa in 1928, he thought he was at the end of the world. He lived in a tent, herding sheep and the remote frontier became a familiar face.

19 CORNET FALLS

Time:	**1/2 hour to the base of the falls**
Distance:	**Approximately 1/4 mile to the base of the falls from the bridge at Cornet Creek**
Elevation Gain:	**Approximately 400 feet**
Maximum Elevation:	**9,200 feet at the base of the falls**
Difficulty:	**Difficult**
Trailhead:	**Aspen Street at Cornet Creek bridge (Jud Wiebe trailhead)**
Trail End:	**Same as trailhead**
Map:	**U.S.G.S. Telluride Quadrangle**

During the summer, this short trail offers a quick, accessible escape from town. In late summer, raspberries are abundant along the creek bed. As with the mountain weather and seasons, these falls change character continuously; sometimes they are a fine spray, and sometimes a thundering boom. Often a nice pool lies at the base of the falls. At almost any time of year, these inspiring falls are worthy of investigating.

The hike in the summer is a short scramble above the creek bed. It is well worth the escapade, but wear well-gripping shoes and prepare for a few hands-on moves. This short, steep trail requires careful footing as it crosses avalanche, mud, and rock slide paths. Due to the steep traverse with poor footing, I think this is a difficult hike. The steep drainage leads to a waterfall cascading over red cliffs. In winter months, Cornet Falls freeze into a solid ice cone. Ice climbers have experienced the entire falls crashing into oblivion. Luckily, no climbers have been killed, but there have been some debilitating injuries. You can see these frozen falls from the top of Coonskin.

The hike to Cornet Falls begins at North Aspen Street in Telluride, where the steel bridge crosses the creek to start the Jud Wiebe Trail. Stay east of the creek (on the right side going up) and follow the path that climbs along the creek. Watch your step over loose rocks and unmarked obstacles.

The cables hanging above the creek are the remnants of a bridge that held two pipes for the town's water supply. One pipe carried water from Mill Creek along the Waterline Trail, and the other transported water from the falls. Today, the water system has been restructured and these pipes are obsolete.

Cornet Creek has flooded occasionally. One local old timer remembered the July 31, 1969, flood as it engulfed her home. It was in the afternoon and her four small children were napping. She heard a sound like a jet and a neighbor yelled "Cornet Falls! Cornet Falls!" From her metal mine shack below the falls, the mother saw a wall of mud with trees in it coming down Aspen Street. When the back of her house caved in, a barefoot neighborhood boy helped carry her four children to safety.

"Dutch George" had the first water business in the area. He used water from the spring at the foot of Cornet Creek. He carried 2.5 gallon oil cans hung around his neck, on each side, and he delivered water to the businesses on Main Street for ten cents a can.

On May 5th, 1900, in the *San Miguel Examiner*, an article about a hermit who lived in Cornet Basin appeared: "The Old Man who has Long Been Known to the People of this City as the Old hermit of Cornet Basin, Passed away Last Sunday Evening. Last Sunday evening at a late hour the dead body of 'Father' Shepherd was brought down from his cabin in Cornet Creek basin and taken to the Morgue of Glenn's undertaking establishment to be prepared for burial.

For the past seventeen years the old man has lived a life of almost utter seclusion in his little log domicile, his only companion and associate being a

Trailhead to Cornet Falls

dog. At intervals as necessitated it, he journeyed down to town to procure a small stock of provisions and returned to his recluse again. He was an eccentric character and avoided largely any association with his fellow man, and but little of his past was known. The fact that he was born in Ohio, at Lockland, Hamilton county in 1820, that he crossed the plains in 1859 to Salt Lake City with an ox team, and that he landed in Telluride in 1883 is about all the information that was known of him. He claimed to have had a revelation, in some manner, of a fabulously rich gold vein in the mountain where he lived, and he has spent the past seventeen years prospecting over the hill and digging holes in search of it, always confident that he would soon find it.

The old man had lain in his cabin sick and helpless for a week before he was found, and only lived a short time after assistance reached him. Manager McCall of the Western Union telegraph office and Lester Latch were last Sunday afternoon strolling over the hills up Cornet Creek, and when they neared the old cabin the dog rushed out to them and by pitiful whinings and almost human manifestations, making louder his demonstrations when they attempted to proceed in another direction, induced them to go with him to the cabin. There they found the old hermit in his rude bunk, with no fire, the door open, and almost unconscious. They at once brought word to town and Dr. James went up to attend the old man, but found him beyond human aid, and at six o'clock he died.

During the past three or four years the county has lent Mr. Shepherd some financial aid, as has also N.T. Mansfield and others, although his wants were few."

౨౧

20 DEEP CREEK

Time:	**Plan on approximately 4 hours from either direction.** To start at Mill Creek, drive west of Telluride on Highway #145 to the gas station and turn right, south, on the dirt road. Drive up the road to the water treatment plant and park and take the trail west, left. To go from west to east, drive up Last Dollar Road and turn right just before the airport. Go about a mile and park at the corral.
Distance:	**8 1/2 miles to Cornet Creek; 6 miles to Mill Creek from the corral trailhead beyond the airport on Last Dollar Road. 4 1/2 miles to the West Fork of Deep Creek.**
Elevation Gain:	**1,672 feet from town**
Maximum Elevation:	**10,478 feet at the ridge between Eider Creek and Remine Creek**
Difficulty:	**Moderate**
Trailhead:	**There are three possibilities for starting this trail.** Going east to west: 1) You can take the west end of the Jud Wiebe, walk from Cornet Creek to Butcher Creek and do the Waterline Trail to Mill Creek. This will add 2 miles to your hike. 2) Eliminate those two miles by starting at the water treatment plant. Take the Mill Creek Road, outside of town by the Brown Homestead, across from the gas station to Mill Creek, at the water treatment facility. 3) Going west to east, you will start from Last Dollar Road, one mile beyond the airport at the corral.
Trail End:	**Same as trailhead**
Maps:	**U.S.G.S. Telluride and Gray Head quadrangles**
Forest Service Trail:	**#418**

This is a wonderful hike and is especially good for early spring and late fall because of its low elevation and sunny exposure. In 1995, the trail was good on November 17.

If you are looking for a leisurely day's saunter, something not overly exerting, you will have a wonderful time in any direction on any portion of this trail.

This trail can be somewhat confusing since it is located between other trails. (The Whipple Mountain Trail is to the east of the Deep Creek Trail. The Sneffels Highline comes in from the south to meet the Deep Creek Trail. The Jud Wiebe meets the Deep Creek Trail at Butcher Creek. The straight east-west traverse which ends at Mill Creek is the Waterline Trail.) The west fork of Deep Creek itself starts in the Sneffels Wilderness to the northwest of Ruffner Mountain. The origin of the creek can be reached from the Whipple Mountain Trail, starting on top of Last Dollar Road, or from the Deep Creek trailhead which is located lower on the Last Dollar Road at the corral, which is a mile from the Telluride Airport. The entire Deep Creek Trail, from Butcher Creek to the origin of Deep Creek, is twelve miles. To avoid confusion, look at the Forest Service and the U.S.G.S. maps indicated for each trail.

In 1995, the U.S. Forest Service made a land trade with the Aldasaro family to change the trailheads for the Whipple Mountain and the Deep Creek trails. The new legal trailhead is one mile from the turnoff to the Telluride Airport and includes forty acres of land surrounded by development on Last Dollar Road. Technically, this is in the middle of the Deep Creek Trail. Starting at the corral, switch backs wind up to the road cut along the irrigation ditch, fed from the East Fork of Deep Creek, where you go left, west, along an irrigation ditch. (Do not go right on this road which is access to private property.) If you wish to go to the origin of the creek itself, Deep Creek, which is west, below Ruffner Mountain, keep going left on the road. From the corral to the west fork of Deep Creek is three hours round trip.

This is a relatively moderate hike because the elevation gain is minimal. The views are incredible and particularly dramatic in the fall when the colors are changing. The trail itself is straightforward and obvious most of the way.

Starting from the Mill Creek water treatment plant, the trail is marked by wooden signs. From Mill Creek the gradual ascent to the meadow in lower Mill Creek Basin where the trail goes left, west, toward Deep Creek takes approximately half an hour. Views of Dallas Peak, Gilpin Peak, and upper Mill Creek are outstanding. From here, the trail switchbacks beyond the Sneffels Highline Trail to its highest point, the ridge separating Mill Creek and Eider Creek, descending to Eider Creek after crossing a small meadow.

This was an old game trail, used today by horses, bikers, and hikers. The trail traverses around several aspen covered ridges and crosses slide paths and small stream beds below Campbell Peak and Iron Mountain. As the trail cuts through the aspen forest overlooking the Mountain Village and Lawson Hill, columbine, elderberry, and larkspur are abundant.

Eventually, you pass a sign in a meadow which says "Deep Creek Trail and Mill Creek 4 miles." Bring your camera to this picnic spot, where views of Imogene Pass, Emma, Greenback, Lizard Head, the ski area, Sheep Mountain, and the Wilsons are spectacular. Go a short distance down the road that cuts through here and take the trail cut to the west which is indicated by a sign to Deep Creek. Stay on the traverse and do not drop down to the left where a trail cut leads to private property.

As the road toward Deep Creek cuts downward, Basque graffiti is evident on the aspens. Shepherds spent considerable time in the woods here. Beyond this, the sign "Deep Creek 2 miles" points toward the trail. After a considerable descent, the trail comes out by an old irrigation ditch on a roadbed. Continue left, heading east on the road for a short distance and then drop down to the right. Eventually, you will come out at the corral.

If you want to walk to the origin of Deep Creek, go west on the roadbed which follows the irrigation ditch. You may need to look around for a good place where the trail crosses the creek. Afterwards, it climbs up to a junction with the old Iron Mountain Road. Go north on the road, downhill, about half a mile to a signed junction. The Deep Creek Trail heads right, north-west, leading to the Whipple Mountain Trail by traversing around the south facing hillside into the west fork of Deep Creek. The trail stays high on the oak covered hillside for a short distance before dropping down into the drainage. It follows benches with aspens to a rocky gully crossing which is an intermittent tributary of Deep Creek. The trail heads up the creek through several grassy benches and meanders up the narrowing drainage. The trail follows the creek up through a few small meadows before starting to climb a steep hillside along an old road grade. At the top of the hill, the trail traverses a meadow and leaves the creek drainage heading uphill. This is where the Deep Creek Trail meets the Whipple Mountain Trail. You can continue right, to the origin of the creek below Ruffner Mountain, or go left toward Whipple Mountain.

This hike brings to mind the Walt Snodgrass story. Walt lived in Telluride on east Pacific Street in the red light district and was known as a local "character." He let his white beard grow each year before he an-nounced that he was going in for his annual shave. At times, he rolled one hundred dollar bills which were seen sticking out of his shirt pocket.

In September, 1948, as the aspens turned, two Missouri men came to town and asked about the Mountain Flower Mine. Walt Snodgrass, then a mere seventy-two, loved to talk and show "outsiders" around. He volun-teered to take the men to the mine. They drove with Walt to Deep Creek and one man waited in the car while the other walked the nearly two and a half miles to the mine. While returning from the mine in the dark, Walt supposedly dropped dead on the trail. The Missouri man said he built a campfire and spent the night be-side Walt's body. He walked back to the car after sunup and he and

Deep Creek/Sheep Creek trailhead at Mill Creek

his partner called Tom Mahoney, the sheriff at that time. A search for Walt's body and signs of the campfire was made and neither found. Strangely, the town Marshal disappeared at the same time that Walt took his last walk in the woods. Some old timers say the Marshal had gone by an alias and that he was really Jesse James. Interesting rumors roam these hills!

Remine Creek was named after the brothers, William W., a Confederate soldier of Company C., 10th Calvary; and Lindley M., a Union soldier of Company G., 13th Calvary. Their graves are marked at the Lone Tree Cemetery in Telluride.

Lindley, known as Lon, came to Telluride in 1873. He was drafted with his brother into the Confederate Army. Lon deserted and joined the Union. The brothers had not spoken in ten years when Bill was gored to death by a bull in the Last Dollar area. In 1887, Lon was a prospector and he had a "shelter of sorts" at the fork of Deep Creek Road. He and his partner made a rich strike that they sold for $40,000. Lon ordered a new home to be built east of Remine Creek. It was a block house with hewn, spruce logs, built without nails. After the house was done, Lon went back to Kentucky for his bride. Conflicting stories represent his disillusion. One is that his fiancee was already married. Another is that he returned alone and disappointed after she had wanted to bring her mother and he had objected.

Known as the "old hermit," Lon's hospitality was legendary. Harold Ramsey remembered kids going by Lon's shack to see what treasures he had found. Harold saw Lon, under five feet tall, tear off a piece of canvas from his shack and take a bar of soap to the creek for a bath. Another old timer remembered Lon making walking sticks for all the kids. The lonely and the thirsty came through his door where a tin cup hung beside a barrel of liquor. Each spring, Lon sought the lost mine of Mill Creek, spending his funds on blasting powder, starting one tunnel after another. A bench beside his cabin was the idling place of two generations of children. No child left his place empty handed. Mothers sent Lon fresh baked goods. His cabin was furnished from the city dump. He was known as a pack rat and had so much junk at his shack that he had to move out into a nearby cave. One old timer remembers her childhood visits to Lon's "dug out," a cave-like hole dug out of the hillside. Lon was reported to have had the largest wind chime in the world, his fence. Lon hung tin cans and badger hides around on log poles to make noise. "When the wind blows, the cans rattle and make me think someone is around and it's music and company for me," he was reported to have said. He had a fence on top to keep the burrows off his roof. The place had no windows and Lon used what was called a "bitch" for light. Grease or lard was placed in a dish and fabric was rolled tightly, used as a wick. It was saturated by the oil or grease and would burn a long time. Lon's bed consisted of aspen poles covered with pine boughs, covered by grass and a few smoky gunny sacks. This was covered by dirty blankets and comforters. Horses could barely keep up with Lon as he climbed the steep mountainsides. He looked grim most of the time, but was remembered for his friendly soul, his innocent eyes and his kindness.

21 IRON MOUNTAIN ROAD

Time:	**3 hours round trip**
Distance:	**Approximately 5 miles round trip**
Elevation Gain:	**Approximately 1,400 feet**
Maximum Elevation:	**10,400 feet**
Difficulty:	**Moderate**
Trailhead:	**The corral on Last Dollar Road, approximately 1 mile beyond the airport**
Trail End:	**Same as trailhead**
Map:	**U.S.G.S. Gray Head Quadrangle**
Forest Service Trail:	**#418**

This is a pleasant walk up an old unmaintained road. The trail starts at the trailhead for the Deep Creek and Whipple Mountain trails at the corral beyond the airport on Last Dollar Road. It winds up to an old road along an irrigation ditch, passing the sign pointing east to "Mill Creek 6 miles — Whipple Mountain 3 miles" west and after about forty-five minutes crosses a fork of Deep Creek. The creek crossing can be tricky. Try heading upstream a bit and look for a safe place to cross. The road continues heading upstream briefly and then back, heading toward Whipple Mountain and merges with the Iron Mountain Road.

Iron Mountain Road is neither marked nor maintained. Go right, heading west at the Iron Mountain Road merge point. You can see a fairly new pipeline across the canyon, heading up the creek. It is about fifteen minutes of uphill walking on this road, crossing a small talus slope, to a view of the falls coming down the canyon ahead.

For a moderate workout, just walk an hour and a half from the start and turn around when you see the falls. You can continue walking into the basin above the falls on this road which eventually becomes a trail, for a longer hike. The views of the Wilsons and Lizard Head from this road are amazing when you turn around and come down. This is a great fall hike when the colors are ablaze. You will find less traffic here than many of the other more popular trails.

Iron Mountain Road

──**22** JUD WIEBE TRAIL──

Time:	**1 to 2 hours round trip**
Distance:	**2.7 miles round trip**
Elevation Gain:	**Approximately 1,200 feet**
Maximum Elevation:	**9,800 feet**
Difficulty:	**Moderate**
Trailhead:	**Aspen Street at the Cornet Creek bridge**
Trail End:	**Tomboy Road and Oak Street**
Map:	**U.S.G.S. Telluride Quadrangle**

The Jud Wiebe Trail, linking Butcher Creek and Cornet Creek, is an excellent place to start spring hiking as it is one of the first hikes to become clear of snow. Some even hike this trail throughout the winter. Access to this loop can be found either from Aspen Street or Tomboy Road. Starting at Aspen Street is a more moderate climb and recommended in the spring when snow lingers in steep, shaded areas.

At the north end of Aspen Street, the trail begins at the bridge that crosses Cornet Creek and heads west, left, among silver spruce, ponderosa, and aspen. It is about a mile, a thirty-minute stroll, to Butcher Creek.

Butcher Creek water was used in the Telluride Brewery, once located on the creek west of the high school. It was reportedly too pure to conduct electricity without the addition of salt.

The road flattens and swings to the right, east, at Butcher Creek. After this flat spot, the trail climbs to "Breakfast Rock," a comfortable overlook where views in all directions are photo-worthy.

From here, the short, steep switchbacks lead to the high point of the trail, to the ridge overlooking the entire valley floor all the way to the La Sal Mountains in Utah, near the Colorado River and the town of Moab. Along this ridge is a spectacular photographic vantage point for unobstructed views of the ski area, Bear Creek, La Junta Basin, Gray's Basin, Ingram, Ajax, and Trico peaks, and Ingram and Bridal Veil falls. The trail levels from here, then drops through the aspens back down to Cornet Creek.

A wooden bridge crosses Cornet Creek, and the trail again climbs briefly to the road at Liberty Bell Flats. Go to the right and climb very briefly on the road that drops steeply to the water storage tank, then return to town on the Tomboy Road.

If you are hiking from Tomboy Road, take the first switchback to the left where the road is generally closed to cars by a steel gate. It is a steep and strenuous walk beyond the water storage tank to Liberty Bell Flats, the first level point. Old timers remember baseball games played between the

Jud Weibe trailhead

Liberty Bell miners and the town teams at the flats.

In the flats is a sign designating the Jud Wiebe Memorial Trail, which drops down through the trees on the left. The trail continues down to the wooden bridge across Cornet Creek, and then climbs moderately to the ridge viewpoint.

From either direction, this is a great hike and a good way to orient yourself to the valley. This hike can be done at a brisk, jogging pace of under an hour or more slowly in approximately two hours. It can be a steady stroll or an aerobic workout. At whatever speed you adopt, the Jud Wiebe trail is a must.

The trail originally served as access to the county pest (probably for pestilence) house. The pest house was built in a flat spot near Butcher Creek in 1901. According to the May 10, 1901 edition of the Denver Times, "The erection of this building was a good move on the part of the authorities and a better location could not have been chosen, as it is an ideal spot and is well isolated from the main thoroughfares." The building was eighteen by thirty-six feet and was used to quarantine contagiously ill people. Old-timers remember smallpox, scarlet fever and diphtheria as the most popular diseases at that time. The building was used for approximately fifteen years, until 1916.

As the Forest Service preserved this trail and made a loop from Butcher Creek to Cornet Creek and the town of Telluride, it was dedicated and named in honor of Jud Wiebe, a Forest Service ranger whose outdoor enthusiasm and good works still mark the area. Jud died of cancer in 1986 after designing the trail with Dave-O Whitelaw. Jud's enthusiasm inspired the Forest Service involvement in recreational service and a whole trail system.

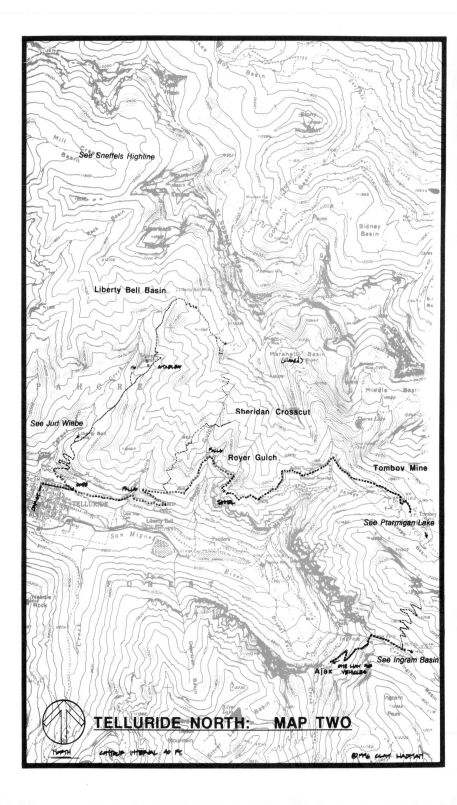

See Sneffels Highline

Liberty Bell Basin

Sidney Basin

Marshall Basin (closed)

Middle Basin

See Jud Wiebe

Sheridan Crosscut

Royer Gulch

Tomboy Mine

FALLS

FALLS

TELLURIDE

FALLS

San Miguel

Pandora

River

See Ptarmigan Lake

FOREST

Ajax

THE WAY FOR VEHICLES

See Ingram Basin

Ingram Peak

TELLURIDE NORTH: MAP TWO

NORTH   CONTOUR INTERVAL 40 FT.

©1996 CLAY WADMAN

───**23** LIBERTY BELL BASIN───

Time:	1 hour to the "Y" where the road goes left to the Stillwell Tunnel and right to Liberty Bell Basin. It is 1/2 hour of steep walking to the basin from this junction.
Distance:	Approximately 2.3 miles to Liberty Bell Basin
Elevation Gain:	2,524 feet; approximately 1,524 feet to the Stillwell Tunnel, add another 1,000 feet to the Liberty Bell Mine
Maximum Elevation:	11,400 feet at the Liberty Bell Mine
Difficulty:	Difficult (steep and aerobic)
Trailhead:	First switchback to the left on Tomboy Road. You can also make a loop with the Sheridan Crosscut Mine located between Owl Gulch and Royer Gulch (see Sheridan Crosscut hike).
Trail End:	Tomboy Road and Oak Street
Map:	U.S.G.S. Telluride Quadrangle

The Liberty Bell Mine is at tree line, approximately 2.3 miles north of Telluride. Plan on half a day for this walk, where remnants of mining history may beguile the curious.

The most direct route from town is to take the first left switchback on Tomboy Road at the metal gate, where the road winds steeply northwest to the town's water storage tank overlooking town and the ski mountain. The hike is continuously steep to Liberty Bell Flats where the Jud Wiebe Trail cuts off to the left, west. Continue straight ahead to the Liberty Bell Mine.

The Liberty Bell Flats once offered summer graze land to dairy animals and livestock and was used as a baseball field for miners living above. The road continues upward, crossing a creek that feeds into Cornet Creek and climbs steeply to a fork. The left fork leads to the Stillwell Tunnel which pipes water to the town's storage tank. The walk takes approximately an hour to this point. It is here at 10,460 feet that the mine's main portal was located.

Continuing to the right at the fork, the road climbs past the old horse stables and cabin ruins, which were situated on the left. The stables were used to keep horses for the miners and their families who rode from town. In 1915-1916, school aged children rode their horses from Liberty Bell to school in Telluride every day.

Beyond these ruins, the road takes a sharp left, and then a right, climbing steeply another mile to Liberty Bell Basin. Elk are often seen in the early mornings or evenings at the upper end of Liberty Bell Basin. If you are still, you may see some dancing through the meadows and hillsides.

A number of ruins in the basin indicate where the upper workings known as "I" level nestled between Greenback Mountain to the northwest and Mendota Peak to the southeast. From the upper workings of the mine, you can return to town just as you came up, or you can continue straight ahead over the ridge at the west end of the basin to Marshall Basin.

To walk to the saddle above Marshall Basin, take the trail at the end of the road and continue walking toward Mendota Peak, staying left at the end of Liberty Bell Basin. Traverse right across the scree, between two obvious rock outcroppings to the ridge. This is an old game and miners' trail that connects the two basins. From here, you can also go to the Sheridan Crosscut Mine. Don't take the trail ahead at the end of the basin; instead, go right, east, on the road. This road ends and you go over the ridge and cross a grassy slope, dropping down to the flat spot below. Cross the eastern creek bed and walk around to the next gulch where the mine is located. (First do this from below, starting at the Sheridan Crosscut. Many have been lost trying to make this loop. Figure it out from each side before you attempt to link the two. See Sheridan Crosscut hike.)

If you plan to use this access to Governor Basin, or to simply look at the ruins of the Sheridan, Mendota, and Smuggler mines, remember that Marshall Basin is off limits, and you will be trespassing if you drop into it.

This is a great walk, and quite challenging for those unacclimatized. So go slowly and take it easy, enjoying the views as you march back in time.

In 1876, W.L. Cornett discovered the Liberty Bell. The mine was developed two years later by the Liberty Bell Gold Mining Company, and during

San Sophia Ridge from the road in Liberty Bell Basin

the next twenty years, $16,000,000 was gained. The Liberty Bell Mine, one of the three largest mines in the area, had one of the biggest payrolls. About 150 men worked in the mine and about half a dozen families lived there. Men worked a ten hour day underground, and half of them walked to town to spend the night with their families. Many rode horses to work from Telluride.

Avalanches were not uncommon at the Liberty Bell Mine, and one year the entire blacksmith shop, everything but the floor, was wiped out. Life was harsh at "I" level. Wind and snow blew through the old wooden siding on buildings and the spring water was stagnant and contaminated. Drinking water was drawn from inside the mine, where one woman luckily escaped a snow slide as she filled her water container.

Shoppers often came down on horses to buy groceries in Telluride and went back up on the tram located at the mill site, by the old stone building at the east of the Lone Tree Cemetery.

In 1902, eighteen people were killed in successive snow slides at the Liberty Bell. The original boardinghouse was located at the upper workings, and on February 28th, 1902, at 7:30 a.m., the first of three avalanches hit the boardinghouse, the tramway station, and the ore-loading house. More would have died, had not this slide missed the old bunk house where the night shift slept. The day shift in the mine also escaped injury.

A rescue party from Telluride dug out seven bodies, when a second slide came down. No one was hurt then, but as the rescue group marched toward Telluride with the dead and the wounded, a third avalanche killed three more and injured five. The dead and the injured were brought into Telluride on improvised sleds made of strips of sheet iron, rolled up in canvas covers with ropes at each end for rescuers to hold. One man in front acted as guide, and two men in the rear acted as brakes. Gravestones in honor of those who died are located to the north in Lone Tree Cemetery.

The original boardinghouse held approximately 100. It burned down around 1930 and the boardinghouse at Stillwell Tunnel was built. The concrete foundation by the Stillwell Tunnel identifies the location of the boardinghouse where old timers witnessed dances as kids. The miners turned the banquet tables upside down and hoisted them to the ceiling. Those tables had about twelve inch sides and were used like playpens. The children were put in them to recline, to sleep, and to observe. Imagine the view of those miners kicking up their heels!

There were also mule barns near the Stillwell Tunnel. The mules were called "Rocky Mountain Canaries" for their high pitched shriek. When they were overloaded, the mule's shrill whistle sounded like a canary. The "canaries" worked day and night, and many saw daylight only once or twice a year.

As you walk these hills, the sounds of drill and hammer and the clatter of horseshoes and hobnailed shoes echo throughout the countryside. The San Juan miner was of an incredible breed whose strength of body and spirit was remarkable.

24 ROYER GULCH

Time:	45 minutes to the falls in Royer Gulch
Distance:	1 1/2 miles to the falls
Elevation Gain:	1,600 feet
Maximum Elevation:	10,400 feet
Difficulty:	Moderate
Trailhead:	Tomboy Road and Oak Street
Trail End:	Same as trailhead
Map:	U.S.G. S. Telluride Quadrangle

Spring is the best time of year to see the falls gushing in Royer Gulch, a mile and a half from Telluride up Tomboy Road. Spring is the only time of year when the twin falls appear. While Imogene Pass is still snow covered and closed, the traffic is minimal.

These falls cascade above the Tomboy Road where old cable lines that accessed the Sheridan Crosscut Mine directly above can still be seen to the west. Be careful here, because spring thaws can induce boulders and avalanche debris to cut loose from above.

At the bend, beneath the falls, wild raspberries flourish at the end of the summer. Beyond the falls, at Social Tunnel, a breathtaking view back to town can be enjoyed. The blasting of that tunnel was a feat of human labor to provide access to Marshall and Savage basins.

The hike starts on North Oak Street at Tomboy Road, the link to Telluride's first mining discoveries in the late 1800s. It is approximately fifteen minutes to the Owl Gulch waterfall. At one time, these falls offered a great water stop for horses en route to the basins above.

Beyond Owl Gulch, the road flattens and offers views of Deertrail Basin, Ballard Mountain, La Junta Basin, the lower ridge of Wasatch Mountain, San Joaquin Ridge, Lena Basin, Gold Hill, Needle Rock, the ski area, and town.

At the end of this flat section, the road bends left, north, into Royer Gulch. Take the time to look at Ingram and Bridal Veil Falls to the east before heading north. Any time of year, this is a sight to behold. For your perspective, the falls are directly below the Sheridan Crosscut Mine. Notice the red sandstone walls to the north in Royer Gulch where the falls cascade. Look left, west, up the last gully before the falls. Here, old tramway lines that serviced the Sheridan Crosscut Mine and the mill in Pandora can be seen.

Be very careful to avoid rock slides, especially in the spring, in this area. The falls are a short lived, spring phenomenon; try to get up there while they are still flowing.

25 SHERIDAN CROSSCUT

Time:	**4 1/2 hours round trip**
Distance:	**Approximately 2 1/2 miles from Tomboy Road and Oak Street to the mine site**
Elevation Gain:	**3,000 feet**
Maximum Elevation:	**11,225 feet at the mine; 12,000 feet at the saddle where you make the loop with Liberty Bell Basin**
Difficulty:	**Difficult**
Trailhead:	**Tomboy Road and Oak Street**
Trail End :	**Same as trailhead**
Map:	**U.S.G.S. Telluride Quadrangle**

One of the things I like about the Sheridan Crosscut is that it is hard to find and little traveled. This is a special hike to me. It's one of the first "off road" hikes surrounding town I discovered. I saw my first elk in the steep grassy meadow above the mine there.

My neighbor, a wonderful little old Italian lady named Mrs.Clementi, worked at the Sheridan Crosscut. I remember Mrs. Clementi gathering wood scraps to start her stove in the early 1970s. I don't think she was even five feet tall, but she worked harder than anyone else in the neighborhood gathering wood and tending her garden. The hike begins on Tomboy Road. Parts of this hike may be off limits, so please respect the property owner's wishes and get permission to do it.

If I make a loop of this hike, I start up Liberty Bell because the downhill from the Sheridan Crosscut is less severe and easier on my knees. If you plan to make the loop with the Liberty Bell Mine hike, walk up the Jud Wiebe above the water treatment plant. (See directions for Liberty Bell hike.) You can also keep going up the Tomboy Road past the first waterfall, at Owl Gulch and walk directly to the Sheridan Crosscut. You can come back the same way. This route takes less time and doesn't involve the steep ascent into Liberty Bell Basin.

To go directly to the Sheridan Crosscut Mine, walk about forty-five minutes up Tomboy Road. After you pass the first waterfall in Owl Gulch, continue up the steep left switchback where the road flattens, heading right, to the east. (For years I hiked from the steep road cut up to the left of Tomboy Road between Owl and Royer Gulch. Currently, landowners dispute this right of way and a chain is drawn across this road with a "No Trespassing" sign posted. Just recently, another "No Trespassing" sign has been posted above as well. This hike may need the property owner's permission to do.)

Today, the acceptable trailhead is below that road. To find this less obvious trailhead, I have counted 325 steps from the top of the steep switchback, just as I start heading east where the road flattens. Look ahead to see trees on both sides of the road, just after an open space on the left. Pass the first small stand of aspens on the left. At the beginning of the next group of aspens, just as the road stretches toward the right and then bends left, out of sight, there is a trail which heads up and left. Stay on this as it zigs up across the open space, traversing the top of the same clearing and continues into the woods where it joins a more pronounced road. Cross the road and keep heading up toward the rock outcroppings above.

Just under the rock outcroppings, turn sharply left, west, where the trail becomes an animal path. You go around the west, left, side of the rock outcrop through the aspens to a ridge and take a sharp right. At this turn, a rocky point overlooks the basin and old tram towers are visible in the red rock across the gully. The trail takes several sharp turns, eventually switching left below three jagged rock outcroppings. You will pass an old gate on your left which kept in livestock. At present, there are "No Trespassing" signs here. (This probably indicates a need to contact the property owner to obtain permission to go further to do this hike.) To your right, a gully overlooks Tomboy Road. The trail comes out in a clearing atop a ridge where you can see the cirque of mountains straight ahead. On the other side of the mountains ahead is Marshall Basin. Look ahead to your right, below the rock outcrop, and you can see the tailings of the Sheridan Crosscut Mine from this ridge. Take time to appreciate the views in all directions.

It takes another twenty minutes to get to the mine from here. Walk straight ahead and gradually drop on the right side of this ridge into the trees. The trail here is hard to find, but keep going and you will eventually find it. You will walk on a faint animal trail over dead, downed trees and eventually cross a creek bed that leads to an open space. Traverse across this to the next creek bed and then cross it, traversing right, east, across loose sliding dirt and fine rock. This scree walk is a bit risky; watch your footing and be careful. Hiking boots with gripping soles are a big help here. Walk left at the end of this section and see the ruins of the Sheridan Crosscut.

You can return to town by the same route or make a loop with Liberty Bell Basin. To connect with Liberty Bell, walk back across the last creek bed and start up the steep meadow. Many get lost trying to make this loop. There is no trail in this meadow, so zig back and forth, angling left, west, toward the trees on the ridge above. It takes about an hour heading northwest to reach the highest grove of evergreens on the ridge where you will connect with the road into Liberty Bell Basin.

If you have started this loop up Liberty Bell Basin (see Liberty Bell hike), ignore the trail heading toward Mendota Peak, stay on the road, going right, east, at the upper end of the basin. Soon you will pass an old mine shaft, some rails, and an old wooden shed built into the hillside. Walk

Track to Sheridan Crosscut (by Don O'Rourke)

to the ridge at the end of this road. Walk down this steep meadow, eventually coming to a trail that takes you across the creek on the opposite side. Sometimes finding this trail is difficult. Keep heading downward and don't cross the creek bed on the other side until you have hit the trail that traverses at the bottom of this clearing.

The first building site at the mine was the old boardinghouse. Among the ruins are an old wood stove and a metal bedspring and a metal safe. My neighbor, Mrs. Clementi, worked as a cook's helper and met her first husband, Nick Matri, at this boardinghouse. Their daughter, Marina Patterson, remembers throwing her toys into the dump there. She also remembers her mother riding a horse to Telluride and walking into Liberty Bell Basin where she visited a woman friend for an afternoon.

Ore was transported by an elaborate system on a double track decline tunnel to Pandora from the Sheridan Crosscut. That tunnel can be seen at the east end of the Telluride valley in the red walls about a quarter of a mile west of Marshall Creek, if you try hard to find it.

In 1936, while the buildings at the Sheridan Crosscut were still in tact, Leighton Patterson, Marina's husband, and his brother Wes, had a contract to get five one ton ore carts off the dump. They wanted to utilize the still existing tram and let the carts down the rocky gulch above Tomboy Road into Royer Gulch. These ingenious, enterprising, young men found a cable across the valley and a windlass, a machine for hoisting, and borrowed some ropes from the tram crew. Leighton and Wes took the carts apart and tied one item at a time to the cable, pulling the carts uphill across the draw. Finally, they dragged the carts down the slide rock. Despite their hard work, they made little money.

This hike offers another perspective and spectacular views of the valley. For a new slant on the same old beautiful sights, try it. (Be aware, however, that permission may be required.)

✣

—26 SNEFFELS HIGH LINE— (Pack Basin-Mill Creek Basin)

Time:	5 1/2-6 1/2 hours from the the Jud Wiebe trailhead at Cornet Creek to the Deep Creek Trail at Mill Creek; add an hour to include the Waterline Trail, which runs between Mill Creek and Butcher Creek; plan on 8 hours for the full loop
Distance:	11 miles from Mill Creek to Cornet Creek; add 2 miles to include the Waterline Trail
Elevation Gain:	3,600 feet from Cornet Creek; 3,000 feet from Mill Creek
Maximum Elevation:	12,200 feet
Difficulty:	Difficult
Trailhead:	Cornet Creek at the Jud Wiebe trailhead on Aspen Street; or Mill Creek, above the water treatment plant
Trail End:	Same as trailhead
Map:	U.S.G.S. Telluride Quadrangle
Forest Service Trail:	#434

This is a hike that I like to do over and over again; it is a good, close to home, workout. If you do this hike without the Waterline Trail, that section which runs from east to west between Butcher Creek to Mill Creek, you will save two miles and an hour's time. However, this involves shuttle arrangements. In either case, be sure to try this one from west to east, from Mill Creek to Cornet Creek as well as from east to west, which is from Cornet Creek to Mill Creek. It is a new hike from each direction.

To begin from the town, you will start at the Jud Wiebe trailhead at Cornet Creek. Stop where the Jud Wiebe Trail turns right, and go left at the "Mill Creek" sign, following the trail across Butcher Creek, then turning right, north, up the creek. You will see wild strawberries as you walk through the aspen forest. The trail climbs steeply through the trees up the Butcher Creek drainage, and after about two hours, while you are traversing a ridge, a spectacular overlook into Mill Creek is presented. Pause here and look across to the terrain ahead. Continue up the switchbacks into Pack Basin where the log remains of an old miner's cabin stand. The trail traverses under cliff bands and large triangular cairns mark the route through a boulder strewn meadow below Greenback Mountain, to the right, east, and Mt. Emma straight ahead.

Pack Basin was misnamed due to a copying error. Originally named Park Basin, the "r" was misread and translated to a "c." And thus the basin was named Pack Basin. If you are extremely quiet and observant, you may see elk in this popular grazing area.

From the saddle, just under Mt. Emma, the highest point of the hike, between Pack Basin and upper Mill Creek Basin, which you can achieve at a steady, fast pace in two hours, the Sneffels Wilderness below Dallas Peak is spectacular. This is an elk calving area, so go quietly, using minimum impact, and be respectful and observant. You may find yourself in waist to shoulder deep wildflowers and the hand hewn log posts that mark the trail may be difficult to see. Plan on another two and a half to three hours to reach lower Mill Creek Basin from the saddle.

At Mill Creek, where you reach a road, you have the option of going left and continuing to Telluride on the level Waterline Trail, or going right, down the road to the parking area below the water treatment plant or all the way to the main highway at the gas station.

To start from Mill Creek, going from west to east, drive up the Mill Creek road to the water treatment ponds. Park there and begin walking on the "Deep Creek Trail." After approximately fifteen minutes, a sign designates the Jud Wiebe Trail ahead. (If you went straight ahead, turning right after crossing Mill Creek, to the Jud Wiebe, you would be walking on the Waterline Trail; this is essentially a section of the Mill Creek Trail as identified by the Forest Service.) Go left. This is identified by the Forest Service as the "Deep Creek Trail." After approximately half an hour from the start, you will walk into a meadow in lower Mill Creek Basin where Mill Creek Falls and Dallas Peak can be viewed. The trail goes left from here,

Pack Basin

away from Mill Creek, climbing up through a series of terraced open meadows. It is about an hour from the start to the sign "Sneffels High Line and Butcher Creek" and "Mill Creek and Deep Creek."

Go right at the sign to Butcher Creek on the Sneffels High Line. You will walk up through a forest on the spine of a ridge, eventually opening to views of the valley, Lone Cone, Little Cone, Dolores Peak, the Wilsons, Ingram, Greenback, and many other stalwart peaks in the area. The treed area to the west, below Campbell Peak is an elk reserve. Keep walking up past mud-spires to the Mt. Sneffels Wilderness and make a long traverse through purple asters, daisies and wildflower profusions into upper Mill Creek, under Dallas Peak.

If you look down through the trees, you can catch a glimpse of lower Mill Creek Falls. As you come out of the forest into the upper basin, you will see the upper falls. Above these falls are incredible picnic spots. I love this area, where, depending on the time of year and conditions, you may cross fifteen streams. Walk up on the grassy knoll ahead, through large rock cairns, traversing across the scree. The scree piles below the ridge at the end of the valley, north of Mt. Emma are evidence of a glacier moving downward. It takes about fifty minutes to the top of the trail at the end of the valley as it crosses over the saddle into Pack Basin. (Plan on three and a half hours to walk from the start to this saddle.)

This trail is a classic. Both basins are strikingly beautiful and worthy of inspection. Be sure that you are in shape and ready for a full day of hiking. Bring insect repellent for offensive deer flies or mosquitoes and plenty of water.

This spectacular walk in varied terrain was an incredible work of love and hard labor by the Forest Service. Where the path crosses the Mt. Sneffels Wilderness area, all the log work was hand hewn because no motorized or mechanized tools are allowed in the wilderness areas. In ten weeks, Doug Wolfe's trail crew, under the direction of trail designer Bill Dunkelberger, sawed, plowed, and blasted their way through the wilds to create a real classic, a wilderness walk worth far more than words can describe. Don't miss this one. Named the Sneffels High Line, this trail is intended to form a link in a network which will go around the perimeter of the Sneffels Wilderness Area.

27 WATERLINE TRAIL

Time:	**2 1/2 hours round trip from Cornet Creek to Mill Creek**
Distance:	**2 miles to Mill Creek (4 miles round trip)**
Elevation Gain:	**Approximately 800 feet**
Maximum Elevation:	**9,700 feet**
Difficulty:	**Easy**
Trailhead:	**Cornet Creek bridge at the start of the Jud Wiebe**
Trail End:	**Same as trailhead**
Map:	**U.S.G.S. Telluride Quadrangle**

The Waterline Trail is an easy walk on level terrain. It climbs from the Cornet Creek bridge to Epees Park, heading west across Butcher Creek and following the course of an old historic waterline. The first section of the trail traverses through red cliffs and open forest with excellent views of Telluride and the ski area. After about a mile, the trail turns north and works its way into the Mill Creek drainage. This section traverses a dense forest and crosses several small streams. You will pass an old wood structure once used as a crude water filter where the water collected in wooden tanks and the sediment settled. Soon after this, the trail reaches Mill Creek. Look upstream at the dam once used as a settling pond.

You can turn around at the bridge at Mill Creek and return to town on the same trail or cross the creek and follow an old road grade down to the water treatment plant. Then take the Mill Creek Road to the highway and the highway back to town. (This is also a popular bike ride. Many riders begin in town on the spur of Highway 145 going west to the Mill Creek Road at the Brown homestead, across from the gas station about a mile out of town. They ride up to the water treatment plant, then take the Waterline Trail back to town.) This is an alternate route to walk, using the bike path.

This short hike is a good, quick workout and offers great views for contemplation or photography. It can be done as a part of the Sneffels High Line hike or the Deep Creek hike or simply by itself.

28 WHIPPLE MOUNTAIN

Time:	**3-4 hours**
Distance:	**Approximately 5 miles**
Elevation Gain:	**1,000 feet from the west (starting at the parking area near the top of Last Dollar Road); 2,600 feet from the east (starting from the corral near the airport)**
Maximum Elevation:	**Approximately 11,600 feet**
Difficulty:	**Moderate**
Trailhead:	**To go west to east, start at the parking area on the last switchback on the east side of Last Dollar Pass. To go east to west, start at the trailhead one mile east of the airport on Last Dollar Road; this is also 1/2 mile south of Sheep Creek, where a corral and a parking area are found.**
Trail End:	**Same as trailhead**
Maps:	**U.S.G.S. Gray Head, and Sams quadrangles**
Forest Service Trail:	**#419**

Plan on an extra hour to do the shuttle for this hike. You can drive down valley to Deep Creek, where the airport road meets Highway 145 across from the maintenance shed. Or take the airport road above Society Turn approximately one mile to the corral where the trailheads for Deep Creek and Whipple Mountain are located.

This is a great hike from either direction. I prefer going from east to west; the downhill is shorter and less painful on my knees. This is a gradual uphill, a fairly mellow hike. From the trailhead, the trail switchbacks and ends up on a road leading to the creek crossing and then Iron Mountain Road. Keep following this road, left, downhill, the Whipple Mountain Trail is ahead.

The trailhead is off the road, heading right, west. Look for the sign posts through the terraced meadows. At times, the trail is faint so continue heading upward and left, watching for the diagonal slashes on the trees. You will traverse under a rocky ridge line heading left toward Whipple Mountain above the scree ahead. Views of the valley, the ski area, and the mountains surrounding are spectacular from this trail. It is possible to reach the top, where the Mount Sneffels Wilderness ends, in two hours from the start. Walking down from here to the parking area takes less than an hour.

Looking west from Whipple Mountain Trail

From the other direction, heading west to east, the trail climbs to the pass north of Whipple Mountain, gaining elevation in short switchbacks. Westerly views of the La Sal Mountains in Utah are photo-worthy as the trail climbs through aspen groves to the saddle between an unnamed peak and Whipple Mountain. When the trail drops into the West Fork of Deep Creek, views of Ruffner's rocky points and beautiful rock walls are quite impressive. The descent leads down a drainage where you eventually hit the Iron Mountain Road. Continue toward Mill Creek to the trailhead on Last Dollar Road one mile beyond the airport.

The Whipple Mountain Trail is a part of a trail system once known as the Government Trail, built during the Depression. This is a great fall hike while the colors are changing. It is accessible longer than many because of its southern exposure.

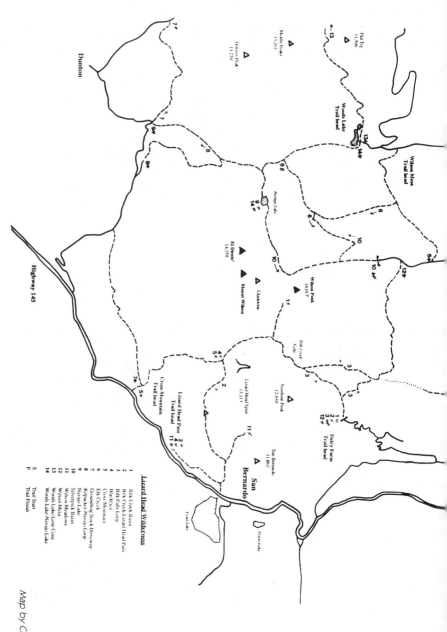

Map by Clay Wadman

29 BILK CREEK BASIN

Time:	7 hours
Distance:	Approximately 10 miles round trip
Elevation Gain:	Approximately 3,000 feet
Maximum Elevation:	12,068 feet at the unnamed lake below Wilson Peak
Trailhead:	On the road beyond the dairy farm on Sunshine Mesa, park at the gate.
Trail End:	Same as trailhead
Difficulty:	Difficult
Maps:	U.S.G.S. Gray Head and Mount Wilson quadrangles; Trails Illustrated Topo, 141, Silverton, Ouray, Telluride, Lake City
Forest Service Trail:	#505 Lizard Head Trail

Add another hour and a half to your time to include the drive to the trailhead and back for this hike. From Telluride, drive down Keystone Hill on Highway 145 and turn left on the Ilium road, passing the gravel plant, continuing to the church camp where you will turn right at the bridge. Cross the South Fork of the San Miguel River and drive up the Sunshine Mesa Road. Go left at the Y ahead and take the road to Wilson Mesa and Lizard Head trails. After you have passed the old dairy farm, park at the gate crossing the road. Start walking up this road, #623.

This is a great walk by creeks, streams, and waterfalls, ending at an unnamed lake below Wilson Peak. Walk about fifteen minutes up road #623 before passing the sign to the Wilson Mesa Trail on your right. Continue on the road beneath Magpie Gulch, looking up at Wilson Peak as you walk along Bilk Creek. Huge avalanches have run through here depositing rocks and trees in their path. After walking forty-five minutes to an hour, you will cross Bilk Creek at the Morningstar Mine. (Here is a nice loop to your right, north, going back down on the other side of the creek. See Lower Bilk Creek Loop.)

Continue to the left, south, walking up along the creek beyond the old cabin and trailer. The trail winds upward through the trees beside the creek into the Lizard Head Wilderness. (Log jams may remain amidst thick snow deposits in the creek.) The trail climbs more steeply toward the lower falls among a profusion of berry bushes. It is about two hours from the start to the open meadows in upper Bilk Basin.

In another fifteen minutes, the trail reaches the road which crosses the creek, going left, south, toward Lizard Head. (This is also the Lizard Head

Dairy Farm on Sunshine Mesa

Trail.) Take the less traveled road to the right, and near the top is a meadow below a small lake. The lake is a great picnic spot where it is possible to view climbers on Wilson Peak.

From the lake you can continue up to the ridge above Navajo Basin to climb Wilson Peak to your right, north, or Gladstone and Mount Wilson to your left, south. Use the same route on this road to return to the trailhead. Watch carefully as you walk down the road, as it is overgrown and easy to get off-route. Take your time and enjoy views of Gladstone Peak, Sunshine Peak, Lizard Head, and the alpine meadows ahead and below.

—**30** BILK CREEK TRAIL—
to Lizard Head over Blackface

Time:	**7-9 hours**
Distance:	**Approximately 11 miles; nearly 5 miles from the start of Bilk Creek Trail to the junction with Lizard Head Trail**
Elevation Gain:	**Approximately 2,500 feet**
Maximum Elevation:	**12,147 feet at the top of Blackface**
Trailhead:	**Sunshine Mesa trailhead, at the end of the Sunshine Mesa Road, see Bilk Creek Basin hike**
Trail End:	**Lizard Head trailhead or Cross Mountain trailhead on Highway 145 beyond Trout Lake**
Difficulty:	**Difficult**
Maps:	**U.S.G.S Gray Head, and Mount Wilson quadrangles**
Forest Service trails:	**Road #623 to #505 Lizard Head**

This is a beautiful day's excursion, and the flowers on this walk are exquisite. Look for violets, hellebore, onions, and light pink Indian paintbrush among others. This is also a good hike to do with someone willing to start at the other end and to trade cars. This makes the shuttle much easier. Plan to meet for lunch below Lizard Head, where everyone will have walked approximately half way, three and a half hours.

To start on Sunshine Mesa, follow the same directions to the trailhead used for the Bilk Creek Basin hike, walking up the road above the creek where elderberry, raspberry, and monks hood, among other outrageous wildflower varieties, adorn the trail. The trail climbs steeply above Bilk Creek, passing waterfalls and several avalanche paths, crossing Bilk Creek by an old cabin and a railroad car at the Morningstar Mine. Be respectful of private property and stay on the trail.

As the trail enters the wilderness, the Lizard Head Trail begins a series of steep switchbacks up past dramatic cliff-lined waterfalls, entering thicker woods and traversing to a more open middle basin. After crossing a small creek, the trail switchbacks up again through willows to timberline and a junction with an old mine road. Lizard Head Trail crosses a cascade to the left. (The road to the right climbs up beneath Wilson Peak and into Navajo Basin.) At the post below Lizard Head, go left, toward Lizard Head. The trail

Old homestead on Sunshine Mesa

traverses under Gladstone Peak and into upper Bilk Basin, dropping down past a small pond to cross Bilk Creek. Then it climbs another set of switchbacks to a saddle and the forest boundary under Lizard Head Peak and Cross Mountain where it meets the Cross Mountain Trail. The Cross Mountain Trail leaves the Lizard Head Trail below, south of the saddle. From the start on the Bilk Creek side, it is approximately four hours to this point.

To continue to the Lizard Head trailhead, you walk toward Blackface following the Lizard Head Trail. From the Blackface side, it is a little over three hours to the ridge above the no-named knob. To avoid lightning, be off Blackface before noon. It is about thirty minutes to the top of Blackface from the meadow below Lizard Head, about an hour and a half from the top of Blackface to the parking area at Lizard Head.

⌐

31 LOWER BILK CREEK LOOP
- Bilk Falls

Time:	**3 hours to make a leisurely loop**
Distance:	**Approximately 5 1/2 miles**
Elevation Gain:	**Approximately 1,400 feet**
Maximum Elevation:	**10,600 feet at the second falls**
Trailhead:	**On the road beyond the dairy farm on Sunshine Mesa, park at the gate**
Trail End:	**Same as trailhead**
Difficulty:	**Moderate**
Maps:	**U.S.G.S. Gray Head and Mount Wilson quadrangles**
Forest Service trails:	**#505 Lizard Head Trail; #421 Wilson Mesa Trail**

Add another hour and a half to your time to include the drive to the trailhead and back for this hike. Follow the same directions for the Bilk Creek Basin hike; park at the gate after the old dairy farm. Walk ten minutes up this road, which is identified as #623, to the Wilson Mesa Trail where you turn right, west, into the trees to begin the loop. Walk half an hour as the trail winds downhill through the forest and open spaces to cross Bilk Creek. Continuing along the Wilson Mesa Trail, look behind you, to the north, at the spectacular view and another perspective of Campbell Peak. Soon you will come to a trail crossing. (If you continue straight ahead, six miles, you will reach the Silverpick Road.)

Take a left, heading south, up Bilk Creek on the Lizard Head Trail. You will be crossing several meadows along the creek. (This was the original trail to the mine. It provided a direct route from John and Goldie Reece's homestead on Wilson Mesa. The trail was also referred to as the "Government Trail.") Then the trail starts to climb steeply, following Bilk Creek upward, crossing several drainages and avalanche paths, around a large waterfall and cliffs. This is the first waterfall shown on the map at 10,026 feet.

Avalanches have torn apart the hillside in this area beneath Magpie Gulch where the Morningstar claims initiate. The Forest Service does a good job of trail clearing, but beware in early hiking season, debris on the trail may be significant. Even after clearings, it is tough going for horses in this area. Plan on an hour and a half to reach the Morningstar Mine ruins from the Wilson Mesa trailhead.

Most of the mines in the area were patented in 1892. A patent allows fee simple ownership on public lands. Unpatented claims are like leases. Regulations were strict in operating this mine, no one under twelve was allowed to work underground.

Continue upward through the trees behind the cabin and mine car for another mile on the trail to the next falls on the map. Come back to this point and cross the creek and walk down the road to complete this loop on the road.

John and Goldie's grandson, Dennis Reece, remembers blasting through the cliffs to build the road in the 1940s.

Avalanche debris

32 BLACKFACE/ LIZARD HEAD TRAIL

Time:	**2 1/2 hours to the summit of Blackface from the Lizard Head trailhead**
Distance:	**6 miles to the juncture with the Cross Mountain Trail**
Elevation Gain:	**Approximately 2,300 feet**
Maximum Elevation:	**12,147 feet**
Difficulty:	**Moderate**
Trailhead:	**Lizard Head Pass parking area at top of pass on Hwy. 145, above Trout Lake**
Trail End:	**Below Lizard Head Peak, at the San Juan National Forest boundary, at the juncture with the Cross Mountain Trail**
Map:	**U.S.G.S. Mount Wilson Quadrangle; Trails Illustrated Topo 141, Silverton, Ouray, Telluride, Lake City**
Forest Service Trail:	**Lizard Head Trail #505**

The hike up Blackface Mountain offers 180 degree spectacular views of: Trout Lake, Sheep Mountain, Yellow Mountain, and Vermilion Peak to the south and east; Sunshine Mountain, Lizard Head, Wilson Peak (14,017 feet), Gladstone Peak, and Mount Wilson (14,246 feet), to the north and west.

The Lizard Head Trail begins on Highway 145 just south beyond Trout Lake and climbs up the spine of Blackface. The trail contours under Blackface Mountain through aspens for about a mile overlooking Lake Fork Valley and Trout Lake. This ridge walk can be extremely hazardous in inclement weather. Lightning's ferocity is more common after noon, so plan to be off this ridge before mid day.

From the summit of Blackface, the Lizard Head Trail continues down to a

Pond below Blackface on route to Wilson Meadows

saddle between Lizard Head and Wilson Creeks. After crossing the saddle, the trail climbs steeply up the northeast face of an unnamed knob on the ridge extending down from Lizard Head Peak. The trail climbs up through tundra above timberline and reaches the ridge and the forest boundary, traversing under Lizard Head peak to a junction with the Cross Mountain trail to the left, south, or the Bilk Creek Trail to the right, north. Follow the Cross Mountain Trail four miles down to Highway 145 or go up to a junction with the Bilk Creek Trail which winds down to the Morningstar Mine. It is also possible to do a loop, taking the old railroad grade east of Cross Mountain Trail back to the Lizard Head Trail.

Elk are often seen in the area, particularly in Wilson Meadows below. Pica and marmots are found in the slide rock and ptarmigan in the bushy areas as well. This is a government trail. Where it tops out on the ridge there was once an old cabin. Woodcutters cut a lot of wood in this area for mine props.

ॐ

33 CROSS MOUNTAIN TRAIL

Time:	1 1/2 hours to beneath Lizard Head; 4 to 5 hours to complete the loop
Distance:	9 miles for the full loop
Elevation Gain:	2,000 feet
Maximum Elevation:	12,000 feet on the unnamed knob below Lizard Head Peak
Trailhead:	On Lizard Head Creek, opposite Sheep Mountain, 3 miles southwest of the parking area for Lizard Head trailhead on Highway 145 heading toward Rico from Telluride
Trail End:	Same as trailhead or to make a loop, at Lizard Head trailhead 3 miles closer to Trout Lake
Map:	U.S.G.S. Mount Wilson Quadrangle; Trails Illustrated Topo #141 Silverton, Ouray, Telluride, Lake City
Forest Service Trail:	#637

This trail heads north toward Lizard Head and soon passes the Groundhog Trail, also known as the Highline Stock Driveway. It is less than an hour's walk through the forest to the Lizard Head Wilderness boundary. The trail winds up and out of the trees on black soil to underneath Lizard Head where it joins with the Lizard Head Trail, heading left, northwest, to Bilk Creek and right, southeast, over Blackface to the parking area by Trout Lake. It is about an hour and a half walk to this point beneath Lizard Head.

To make the loop over Blackface, traverse to the right, under Lizard Head and continue walking on the trail, which gradually winds down beyond the wooden posts ahead, taking a sweeping left and then back to the right below the steep hillside ahead. (In snow covered conditions, I have walked straight across this open space to the opening in the bushes and tumbled down the hillside directly to the trail below. Walk carefully among the loose rock.) Walk across the meadow and back up through the trees to the spine of Blackface.

When you are above the trees on Blackface, take the time to stop and look around. The views of Lizard Head and Cross Mountain are very special from this vantage point. Keep in mind that you have a good hour of exposure while walking on this ridge. It takes about two hours to get down to the Wilson Meadows trailhead sign from under Lizard Head and another hour to the parking area.

꒰꒱

34 ELK CREEK

Time:	3 hours to do the loop with Silverpick Basin; plan on 5 hours for this excursion which includes driving each way in and out of town to and from the trailhead.
Distance:	Elk Creek Trail is approximately 3.6 miles. The lower loop with Silverpick Trail is approximately 5 miles.
Elevation Gain:	Approximately 600 feet
Maximum Elevation:	Approximately 11,200 feet
Trailhead:	Take Silverpick Road 6.8 miles to Wilson Mesa trailhead. Go right and walk along an old mining road beyond a locked gate which denotes the Elk Creek trailhead.
Trail End:	Same as trailhead
Maps:	U.S.G.S.: Dolores Peak, Little Cone, Mount Wilson, Gray Head quadrangles; trail is in the corner of all four maps; Trails Illustrated Topo 141, Silverton, Ouray, Telluride, Lake City
Forest Service Trails:	#407, #421

This trail passes several old roads in the woods where Forest Service posts hold arrows pointing toward the track through a beautiful basin to connect with the Woods Lake Trail at timberline. It is about a fifteen minute walk from the parking area to cross Big Bear Creek, then forty minutes to walk to the Elk Creek trailhead and the Wilson Mesa Trail bulletin board. The Wilson Mesa Trail leaves the road on the right. In less than an additional half-hour the trail passes an old cabin site where a rusted tractor is found and the

Elk Creek

trail switchbacks sharply to the left. Look for gooseberries and currants near the rusted old pot belly stove in this nice flat camp area.

Walk up the road on scree and talus to the Elk Creek Trail sign. There is a faint animal trail through the trees along the creek bed in water-type plants with beautiful flowers between the two creeks. Don't cross Elk Creek, as the trail continues to climb along the edge of the forest to a flat spot. Before a left turn is a sign that indicates Elk Creek and Navajo Lake, which is 4 miles. This is also the continuation of the Elk Creek Trail to the right, as it crosses Elk Creek and is met by the Woods Lake Trail. After leaving the woods and crossing Big Bear Creek, the trail begins traversing a large talus slope and enters a conifer forest. The trail gently switches up along the west side of the creek, passing an old mining cabin, leading to a bench below a steep, unnamed ridge. Then the trail winds west and then south under the ridge to meet the trail to Woods Lake.

To make the loop with Silverpick Road, go left, west, at the Navajo Lake/Woods Lake trail sign and climb up the talus slope on an old road that switchbacks steeply under cliffs and winds above old cabins by Big Bear Creek. You can walk into Silverpick Basin to see the old stone structure which was a boardinghouse built around 1884 and closed in 1910. Walk back down on this road.

35 GROUNDHOG STOCK DRIVE
from Cross Mountain Trail

Time:	**2 1/2 hours of walking; plan on 5 hours total time**
Distance:	**4 1/4 mile, one way**
Elevation Gain:	**Approximately 200 feet**
Maximum Elevation:	**10,600 feet**
Difficulty:	**Moderate**
Trailhead:	**Cross Mountain trailhead off Hwy. 145**
Trail End:	**Dunton road just east of Coal Creek**
Map:	**U.S.G.S. Mount Wilson Quadrangle**
Forest Service Trail:	**#634**

This is a pleasant walk with some incredible views. It doesn't get a lot of use and much of the trail tread has disappeared. (You can get a great workout if you leave a bike hidden at the trail end on the Dunton road and start the walk from the Cross Mountain trailhead off Highway 145 by Lizard Head. The walk takes about two and a half hours and the bike ride back to your car takes an hour, each at a leisurely pace.) Add on to your time an hour and a half shuttle from town. You can also ride your bike on this trail because it is outside the Lizard Head Wilderness.

Access is from Highway 145 on Lizard Head Pass. This section of the trail cuts off from the Cross Mountain Trail. Approximately one quarter of a mile from the trailhead, the stock driveway heads west, to the left, from the Cross Mountain Trail. This section of the trail winds through meadows and spurts of conifer forests where yellow metal signs denoting "Center Stock Driveway" are posted on the trees facing the trail. Minimal elevation gains are achieved as the trail winds up and down. After about twenty minutes, you walk straight across a small meadow. At the second meadow, you veer left viewing Gladstone Peak and Mount Wilson in the distance to the west. There are many secondary paths near this trail due to the scattering of livestock when driven on the route. Beware of many false trails and look carefully for yellow signs, tree slashes, and cairns to mark the route.

At Slate Creek, cross over the bridge and veer left staying close to the creek; do not go up as indicated on the map. (The route doesn't exactly follow the trail indicated on the maps.) Eventually, you'll come to a small post in rocks used as a cairn; don't continue on the most traveled trail there. Go right and walk 150-200 feet and notice a blaze on a ten inch tree on the right of the trail. Go through a small band of trees to a meadow and look for a pole in the

Groundhog Stock Drive Trail

meadow. Watch for yellow "Center Stock Driveway" signs on trees. Continue crossing open parks and meadows with trees scattered until you reach Coke Creek. It can take two hours from the start to reach Coke Creek.

After Coke Creek, look for ruts in the road and walk by the double vertical posts of an old corral toward posts placed in the meadow. It takes about an hour to get to the Dunton road from Coke Creek.

This trail ends on the Dunton road in an open meadow below El Diente Peak across from the 15 m.p.h. sign going in the other direction. This area is called "The Meadows." If you pass the Eagle Creek Road, Forest Road # 471, you have gone too far. The trail end is just before a culvert on Coal Creek.

This trail was used by cattle and sheep men to drive their stock. When the train ran, it enabled people to get their sheep out to the markets on trains. Remnants of the old roadbed still exist along with several sections that make use of designated Forest Service roads.

36 KILPACKER - NAVAJO TRAIL LOOP

Time:	**3 hours to make the loop on the Dunton road with the Navajo Lake Trail**
Distance:	**Approximately 6 miles**
Elevation Gain:	**400 feet from the Kilpacker Trail; 1,000 feet if you start on the Navajo Lake Trail**
Maximum Elevation:	**10,400 feet if you make the loop without going into Kilpacker Basin; 10,800 feet at the falls in Kilpacker Basin**
Difficulty:	**Easy, in general; moderate when you do the complete loop and add the last forty-five minutes of walking back uphill on the road to the car parked at Kilpacker Creek**
Trailhead:	**Kilpacker trailhead on Dunton road; west of Morgan Camp in "The Meadows," at 10,080 feet**
Trail End:	**Same as trailhead or, if you use two cars, at the Navajo Lake trailhead on the Dunton road, at 9,393 feet, one mile north of the Burro Bridge Campground**
Map:	**U.S.G.S. Dolores Peak Quadrangle; Trails Illustrated Topo Silverton 141, Silverton, Ouray, Telluride, Lake City**
Forest Service Trail:	**#635**

Plan on an hour and a half for the drive back and forth from town to do the hike. You will drive on the highway over Lizard Head Pass, turn off on the Dunton road, #207, and continue past the Calico Trail, the homestead, and Meadow Creek. Start at the trailhead off Forest Road #207, in the meadows west of Morgan Camp. The trail follows an old roadbed through conifer forests. Some prefer to start this loop at the Navajo Lake Trail where the elevation is 600 feet higher. This is a wonderful, easy walk across rolling meadows with spectacular views of prominent peaks. Unlike many of the typical steep, straight up Telluride hikes, this one is in the open spaces with little strenuous uphill. The wildflowers are waist deep and water flows abundantly.

You will walk for half an hour to reach the Lizard Head Wilderness, part of a 41,496 acre area created and protected in 1980. Tree fall is evident in this dense forest. Many trees are moss-ridden, appearing more prominent on the north sides, away from the sun.

The loop connection with the Navajo Lake Trail is about an hour's walk. Some prefer this route as access to climb El Diente Peak, Mount Wilson, or Wilson Peak. It is possible to ascend El Diente Peak from Kilpacker Basin, which is up Kilpacker Creek, to the right, east. It is well worth the half hour excursion to see the falls and this lovely lower basin. If the creek is full, you will need to cross on a log positioned across. Beyond the creek crossing, the trail winds back into the basin to a waterfall

Kilpacker Trail

above tree line. The trail continues from the far left, north, in the stand of trees below the waterfall and continues in the scree into the upper basin below El Diente Peak.

To continue the loop, go back out of Kilpacker Creek Basin to the sign and take a right, heading north. The trail goes down, crossing the West Dolores River on another log. Traverse above the creek bed among wild delphiniums and Queen Anne's lace. Eventually, you will meet the Navajo Lake Trail which continues to the right, north, into Navajo Basin. This was an old wagon road constructed into Navajo Basin.

Navajo Lake is the origin of the West Dolores River and an excellent overnight stop. This is a popular camp area and campfires are restricted at the lake, so bring a stove to cook. Please camp at least 100 feet from the lake.

The loop back to the Dunton road continues to the left, south, above the falls where Kilpacker Creek joins the West Dolores River. Soon you will cross the river on another log. The terrain is fairly low angle, almost flat and rolling. From here the views back up into Kilpacker Basin are spectacular. The walk back to the Kilpacker Trail is east, to your left on the road, uphill, adding a moderate rating to this easy hike.

37 NAVAJO LAKE TRAIL

Time:	Plan on 3 hours to reach Navajo Lake; 6 hours to make the Y with Kilpacker Trail
Distance:	Approximately 5 miles to Navajo Lake from the trailhead on the Dunton road. From the lake to the Kilpacker Trail start is about 4.5 miles. The inverted Y is nearly 9.5 miles.
Elevation Gain:	1,716 feet
Maximum Elevation:	11,154 feet at Navajo Lake
Difficulty:	Difficult
Trailhead:	Forest Service Road #535, 1 1/2 miles north of the Burro Bridge Campground; 6 miles off Highway #145
Trail End:	Dunton road at Kilpacker Trail
Maps:	Trails Illustrated Topo 141, Silverton, Ouray, Telluride, Lake City; U.S.G.S. Dolores Peak Quadrangle
Forest Service Trail:	#635

This trail is well traveled by hunters, horses, hikers, and climbers through rolling meadows, glades, and mixed conifer forests along the West Dolores River where two waterfalls cascade into the canyon. The West Dolores River begins in Navajo Basin. If you plan to do a loop with the Kilpacker Trail, the hike is less steep if you start on the Kilpacker Trail from the Dunton road.

The trail starts approximately six miles from Highway 145 on the Dunton road, two miles beyond the Morgan Camp in the Meadows. From the parking area, hike upstream. (Just past the stock bridge on the West Dolores River, the Groundhog Stock Driveway heads left, west.) The Navajo Lake Trail continues to the right on the east side of the river to a log crossing and then heads steeply uphill on the west side in the conifer trees to open, rolling meadows, eventually overlooking a waterfall. It takes a little more than an hour from the Navajo Lake trailhead to meet the Kilpacker Trail. Take the time to enjoy the waterfall coming out of Navajo Basin ahead. The trail undulates, heading upward and views are striking. Plan on another hour and fifteen minutes to intersect with the the Woods Lake Trail. From here, it is another half mile to Navajo Lake, nearly three hours from the start. Beware of lightning in this area. To reach the Woods Lake Trail from Navajo Lake takes about twenty minutes.

The hillsides are alive with flowers interspersed with conifer trees. This is a beautiful walk. It takes about an hour and a quarter to reach the Kilpacker

Navajo Lake

Trail from Navajo Lake. Doing this link, making an upside down Y with the Navajo Lake Trail, gives you a chance to see another trail as well. Some climb El Diente Peak, Mount Wilson, or Wilson Peak from Kilpacker Basin. Be prepared to cross clearings and streams. Although the Kilpacker Trail goes up and down, the elevation is the same at the beginning and the end; 10,000 feet. It takes nearly three hours from Navajo Lake to hike back to the start of the the Kilpacker Trail on Dunton road. The trailhead is located just off the Dunton road in a stand of tall trees.

Not including the shuttle, this is a good five and a half hour hike. To make it easier, begin from the Kilpacker Trail onset, which is about 1,000 feet higher than the start of the Navajo Lake Trail.

38 SILVERPICK BASIN

Time:	**8 hours to loop through Navajo Basin**
Distance:	**Approximately 9 1/2 miles**
Elevation Gain:	**Approximately 3,000 feet**
Maximum Elevation:	**13,200 feet**
Difficulty:	**Extreme**
Trailhead:	**Big Bear Creek below Silverpick Basin. Take Hwy. 145 to Silverpick Road at Vanadium where the road crosses the San Miguel River. Drive 6.8 miles on Road #622 to junction with Road #645, go right two miles. Park at the trailhead where the road is gated, 1 mile past Wilson Mesa Trail.**
Trail End:	**Same as trailhead**
Maps:	**U.S.G.S. Little Cone, Gray Head, Dolores Peak and Mount Wilson quadrangles; Trails Illustrated Topo 141, Silverton, Ouray, Telluride, Lake City**
Forest Service Trails:	**#406, 407, 408, 635**

You can make a nice loop from Silverpick Basin to Navajo Lake and then back over the saddle below Wilson Peak in a long, full day. Silverpick Basin, where the hike begins and ends, has very little vegetation. It is almost entirely slide rock. Looking left and above the basin in the slide rock you will see the old Spanish or Navajo Trail. Mining roads, ruins, shafts, and a tram are scattered throughout the basin. Some campsites are available along the trail, and a loop can be made taking the road one way and the trail the other direction. Bring a fly rod to Navajo Lake, and remember that this loop is well worth the walk, from any direction.

From the Silverpick trailhead, follow the road as it switchbacks up and around the abandoned Silverpick mill. The road traverses around, crossing a stream gully, reaching a junction with a private mining road. The road continues upward through the talus slopes toward the upper basin, following Big Bear Creek. At a junction on a talus slope, one trail heads left for a high traverse below Wilson Peak. Take the other trail which heads right, through talus slopes to another small meadow, following the east side of a ridge to a junction with a larger road and old stone boardinghouse ruins.

You will walk on the Elk Creek Trail to the Woods Lake Trail to the Navajo Lake Trail. To reach the saddle below Wilson Peak from Navajo Lake, it is approximately three miles and takes nearly two hours. This is a strenuous walk and even for someone in good shape, plan on a hike of maximum difficulty. In some years when snow lingers in the high ridge crossings, this hike can be extremely dangerous.

Evert Blackburn owned the property and, in accordance with miner's back country ethic and consideration, Evert left the cabin unlocked and stocked with supplies to help the weary traveler. "I always told him he should lock up the place," Mrs. Blackburn said.

His response was, "Somebody might need a place to get in out of the rain." Evert liked to help others.

The rugged cabin burned to the ground in the early 1970s as a result of "some damned mountain climber's inconsideration. That's how they paid him back," Mrs. Blackburn sighed. The old saloon still stands in the basin there and has been recently used, but today this building is locked and visitors should respect the private property.

Evert's father, Walter, affectionately known as "Dad Blackburn," lived down Bear Creek where he milked cows and packed milk into Silverpick when he was a boy. Five hundred people lived in the basin where the old mill site is located. Three pack strings, consisting of approximately twenty mules each, were sent to the railroad each day accompanied by three guards. Wives spent time hiking, reading, cooking and watching the boys "break in" the mules so they could be used to pack.

Some old timers remember the old toilet there, built out on a platform over the ravine. "When you went in there and sat down, you didn't hesitate. You just went in there and did your business and got out." Some got dizzy walking on the cat walk to the outhouse looking into the canyon below while the wind blew. A long stairway once led into the canyon below. Below the waterfall in the canyon, a cave served as refrigeration and storage for food.

Trout were once abundant and after hours some miners filled old iron skillets with the fish they caught. Mrs. Blackburn remembers the miners sledding on snow shovels at break-neck speeds to arrive in time for dinner. "Their seats got warm," she told me. When she was first married and rode her horse up to Silverpick Basin, a big old hotel range which had a huge warming oven was used in the boardinghouse there. The remains of the old stone boardinghouse are still around.

In 1945, Dad Blackburn died in the Rock of Ages Mine, which overlooks Navajo Lake on the Dolores side. On August 20th, he was cleaning ice out of the tunnel there and had a hemorrhage of the brain. This was considered a very rich mine. One high grader camped with his knapsack, taking out enough ore to live for a year.

ʒ⌒

—**39** WILSON MEADOWS—

Time:	**1 1/2 hour to Wilson Meadows**
Distance:	**Approximately 3 miles one way**
Elevation Gain:	**Approximately 1,000 feet**
Maximum Elevation:	**10,800 feet**
Difficulty:	**Easy**
Trailhead:	**Lizard Head Pass on Highway 145, across from Trout Lake (Begin on the Lizard Head Trail)**
Trail End:	**Same as trailhead**
Map:	**U.S.G.S. Mount Wilson Quadrangle**

The Wilsons are extremely rough mountains with steep slopes, many of which are of over thirty percent grade. Three fourteen thousand foot peaks and fifteen summits above 13,000 feet in elevation exist in the area. This is a good orientation hike in the Wilsons. The hike to Wilson Meadows begins at the first parking area you reach driving from Telluride beyond Trout Lake. This hike is like a European classic sprinkled with wildflowers: wild geraniums, false hellebore, cow parsnip, violets, elderberry, arnia, marsh marigold, mushroom, and columbine, among others.

The trail is in great shape, well maintained by the Forest Service, assisted by Sierra Club volunteers in 1994 and 1995 after significant spring snowfall wrought havoc. Avalanches blocked the trail with tremendous tree fall which went from the Lizard Head Wilderness boundary nearly all the way to the road below. Wilderness regulations prohibit the use of motorized and mechanized devices, so these hearty Sierra Club volunteers guided by Forest Rangers were restricted to using rudimentary tools, like cross cut saws, to clear the trail which climbs under Blackface Mountain through aspen groves and wildflowers.

The hike begins at the trail just behind the restrooms at the top of Lizard Head Pass on Highway 145. A sign marks the trailhead. The Lizard Head Wilderness boundary is at the base of the first set of switchbacks which lead to a small meadow with a juncture of the Wilson Meadows and the Lizard Head trails. Head west, to the right, gradually climbing past a small pond and open meadows. This meadow is a great site for an overnight stay if you camp at least 100 feet away from the water, as required in the back country.

Next, the trail traverses across several boggy clearings and it crosses several small, muddy drainages. After walking about an hour and passing a large campsite on the left, the trail comes into the open by a barren clay shoulder. Follow the clay ridge line down and watch for a post marker. The trail winds in and out of the trees, down to Wilson Creek. After continuing down several clay shoulders and grassy benches, the trail passes through the woods before ending at a log beside shady spruce trees overlooking the meadows.

This is an exquisite picnic spot. Sunshine Peak, Lizard Head, Blackface, and San Bernardo Mountain tower above the meadows here, providing an awesome and inspirational meditative respite.

Until 1974, Wilson Meadows was used as a sheep grazing area. 800 sheep were allocated to this basin. Shepherds packed in 10 by 10 foot walled tents which they moved, along with food and supplies and the "bands" of sheep each week. Occasionally, bear killed sheep; but, generally, livestock and wild game lived in harmony. Since the absence of sheep, some feel the vegetation has gone rank and that the elk population has decreased in this area. This trail once continued toward Sunshine Mountain, connecting with Bilk Creek. In the heavy timber on the east side of the meadows, fish were stocked,

Wilson Mesa Trail

brought in cans to the spruce tree-lined waters of "Clear Lake." This small lake cannot be seen until you are there. One shepherd who has not been in the meadows since the mid 1970s, remembers the nice feeling of being out there sometimes aggravated by the flies and mosquitoes who ate him alive. "If you could put up with the bugs, you could get along well out there," he said.

40 WILSON MESA TRAIL
(Silverpick to Sunshine Mesa)

Time:	**3 1/2 hours for the hike; add another hour for the shuttle**
Distance:	**Approximately 7.5 miles from Silverpick Road to the dairy farm (add 5 miles from Woods Lake)**
Elevation Gain:	**600 feet**
Maximum Elevation:	**Approximately 10,000 feet**
Trailhead:	**Silverpick Road at Wilson Mesa Trail sign**
Trail end:	**Trailhead beyond the Sunshine Mesa homestead**
Difficulty:	**Moderate**
Maps:	**U.S.G.S. Wilson Quadrangle; Trails Illustrated Topo 141, Silverton, Ouray, Telluride, Lake City**
Forest Service Trail:	**#421**

This entire trail, which begins at Woods Lake, is one of the best mountain bike rides in the area. (To do the total trail involves starting at Woods Lake. I have not included the section of the trail from Woods Lake in this edition.) This description involves the walk from Silverpick Road to Sunshine Mesa, beyond the Ilium church camp.

Plan to do a shuttle, leaving your car at the Sunshine Mesa homestead. Drive out to Ilium and cross the creek on the bridge, heading up the Sunshine Mesa road behind the Ilium church camp. Take the left fork to get to the homestead and park at the trailhead by the gate. Then also drive to the bottom of Keystone Hill on Highway 145 and go 6.8 miles up the Silverpick Road, passing the Faraway Ranch turnoff on the right fork, to the Wilson Mesa Trail bulletin board to begin the hike. On one side of the road

Navajo Lake

the trail sign indicates Navajo Lake 8 miles, go the other direction on the Wilson Mesa Trail.

This is a great hike for fall colors. It is open to multi use since it is outside the wilderness. The trail is well traveled through the dense forest, but pay attention and watch for signs to mark the appropriate directions.

Soon after starting, the trail begins rolling up and down, crossing several small drainages in aspen and conifer forests. Wind whipped and beaver gnarled, downed trees are strewn about, occasionally blocking and lining the trail. After passing through a gate in an old log fence, the trail crosses a major tributary of Big Bear Creek and many smaller channels. Leave the gate the way you found it, either opened or closed. Then the forest starts to open as small meadows appear. Notice the skunk cabbage; when it has started to turn, according to old timers' lore, fall is at hand. Some predict the snow will be as high as the skunk cabbage.

The trail climbs to a large meadow where wooden posts below views of Wilson Peak mark the route. At the Lizard Head Wilderness boundary, the trail swings left and drops down to a small pond in the aspens where views of Lizard Head and Wilson Peak grace the background. The trail goes part way around the pond and swings left down into the Bilk Creek drainage. Come out of the forest below Sunshine and Lizard Head at Bilk Creek and continue following the Wilson Mesa Trail to the junction with the Lizard Head Trail, #505. Go left, west, and cross Bilk Creek on an old log bridge and then climb steeply through the trees to the junction with the road before the homestead.

─41 WOODS LAKE ─ LONE CONE

Time:	**Plan on 6 hours with a lunch stop.**
Distance:	**10.5 miles from Woods Lake to the road in Beaver Park**
Elevation Gain:	**Approximately 2,000 feet**
Maximum Elevation:	**11,200 feet**
Trailhead:	**Woods Lake Campground**
Trail End:	**Beaver Park near Lone Cone Guard Station**
Difficulty:	**Moderately difficult**
Maps:	**U.S.G.S. Little Cone, Beaver Park, Dolores Peak, and Groundhog Mountain quadrangles; Trails Illustrated Topo141, Silverton, Ouray, Telluride, Lake City**
Forest Service Trail:	**#426**

This hike requires a shuttle. You can either drive toward Woods Lake from the Fall Creek Road and then take Road #611 to Beaver Park, or drive two miles east of Norwood to the Miramonte Road and take the left turn when the pavement ends to Beaver Park. Either way, plan on an hour and a half to drop off the car at the trail end. I like to do this shuttle the day before.

Just before you reach Woods Lake, from the Fall Creek Road, turn right and take that road to a signed junction. Start walking there. The trail heads toward Woods Lake and up a drainage, then climbs a ridge to the west. The trail follows the ridge through aspens to an old irrigation ditch and continues to the Hughes ditch, which it crosses and begins to climb through aspen covered benches, passing small meadows and a few creeks. This beautiful forest walk is fairly mellow. The trail climbs to openings where the Wilson Peaks and El Diente Peak are seen in the distance. The trail enters the Lizard Head Wilderness and then climbs higher passing meadows and talus fields. It switchbacks to a small pass between Flat Top Mountain and Dolores Peak. The trail follows a ridge and then drops down through a dense forest with a lot of dead wood, small meadows, talus fields, and passes a small lake. It may take about three hours to reach this lake from the trailhead at Woods Lake.

The trail descends through a forest and a timbered ridge, through aspens and meadows and comes to the end of the Lizard Head Wilderness. The trail continues to an opening with a great view of Lone Cone, then to an old road. Follow the trail marker posts and continue, passing a couple of small ponds, crossing a creek. You will walk on and off an old road bed and come to a gate. Follow the sign posts across a meadow and continue, crossing another irrigation ditch. Continue in the same direction through the trees to another gate and descend to Beaver Park Road #611 near the Lone Cone Guard Station.

Three brothers, Albert T., Loren D., and Edwin A. Woods built Woods Lake dam, which was completed in 1901. The brothers' purpose was to build a hydro-electric power plant by fluming water at the mouth of Fall Creek where it would drop down to run a turbine water wheel and power an electric generator, and to run a summer resort.

After a boat dock was built across the dam, Albert and a rancher, Walt Brownley, had a boat race in small wooden boats. Albert flipped his boat and cramped in the icy water. Walt Brownley backed up his boat to tow Albert to shore, while disgruntled gamblers, who had each bet a dollar, watched in dismay.

At the resort, a dance hall was built and Fourth of July celebrations were held. Al Fiett played the fiddle for five dollars and spit a gallon can full of chewing tobacco on nights when he entertained. Bulkley Wells gave the kids silver dollars to find wild strawberries and grasshoppers for him. The Woods brothers also started a sawmill and sold timber until the 1909 Trout Lake flood wiped them out.

∽

42 WOODS LAKE - NAVAJO LAKE

Time:	**2 1/2 hours from Woods Lake to Navajo Lake; 6 hours round trip; plan on forty-five minutes driving each way to and from the trailhead.**
Distance:	**Approximately 5 miles from Woods Lake to Navajo Lake**
Elevation Gain:	**Approximately 1,700 feet**
Maximum Elevation:	**11,154 feet**
Difficulty:	**Difficult**
Trailhead:	**Across from the picnic area, north of Woods Lake**
Trail End:	**Same as trailhead**
Map:	**U.S.G.S. Little Cone and Dolores Peak quadrangles**
Forest Service Trail:	**#406**

This trail extends south from Woods Lake and connects with the Elk Creek and the Navajo Lake trails. You can go into Navajo Basin or Silverpick Basin from Woods Lake. I particularly like the walk from

Woods Lake into Navajo Basin and back.

Drive down valley from Telluride past Sawpit and turn left on the Fall Creek Road. Continue for eight miles to the Beaver Park junction, then continue straight ahead for another mile to Woods Lake. Don't drive all the way to the restrooms and the lake itself. On the left side of the road, across from a picnic area, the trail cuts into the woods.

After you have walked for about half an hour, the trail enters the Lizard Head Wilderness, which is about a mile from the trailhead, and no bikes are allowed. The trail climbs gradually through a dense conifer and aspen forest with occasional switchbacks and four wooden bridged crossings over several small creeks and springs. The trail passes through small meadows with great views of Dolores Peak and Little Cone. After about two and a half miles, the trail climbs more steeply, passing an old log cabin foundation and up to timberline, where an unnamed spring meanders through the drainage. Several excellent campsites are found in this area.

The trail goes to the right under a steep scree ridge above tree line, heading southwest, toward Dolores Peak. This is a rolling traverse across meadows crossing a black, sandy slope that turns left, southeast, toward El Diente Peak and Navajo Lake.

At Navajo Lake, you are below El Diente Peak, to your right, southeast. The peak itself is only visible from the traverse across the sandy slope above, before dropping into Navajo Lake Basin. This pristine lake is at 11,154 feet, 400 feet below the highest point on the trail.

This was the area where "Navajo Sam" accosted hikers for food. His story was one of the most recent episodes of wild west banditry. "Sam" was actually 51 year old Leo Lyyjoke, a logger from Wisconsin, who was "kind of in a bad mood." In October of 1982, when gas rates in Placerville went up, Sam took to the woods. "The American System is coming to an end... I'm Navajo Sam the revolutionary... I'm trying to educate people and fix up the country... about the evils of big business, organized crime, and all war production." Sam claimed "Most people are blaming Reagan, but the American people are partially to blame too." Sam was lonely in the woods. "If there is a lady in Colorado or in the United States that would like to join me, I'd love it... it's a hard, lonely, peaceful life, but the lady would learn a lot about the wilderness, and maybe become a trail bandit."

This big gray-bearded Finnish lumberjack carried a shotgun and a bandoleer with bullets across his shoulder and two pistols. The Forest Service shut down the forest for two weeks, worried that Sam might get in a gun fight with elk hunters. A man hunt for Sam ensued. His capture came about when he was tricked into a handshake to show his gun to two local sheriffs, Bill Masters and Eric Berg, who arrested him. Sam was ultimately let go because those he had accosted were tourists who had left the area, and no one was around to press charges. Sam also moved on and his whereabouts are unknown.

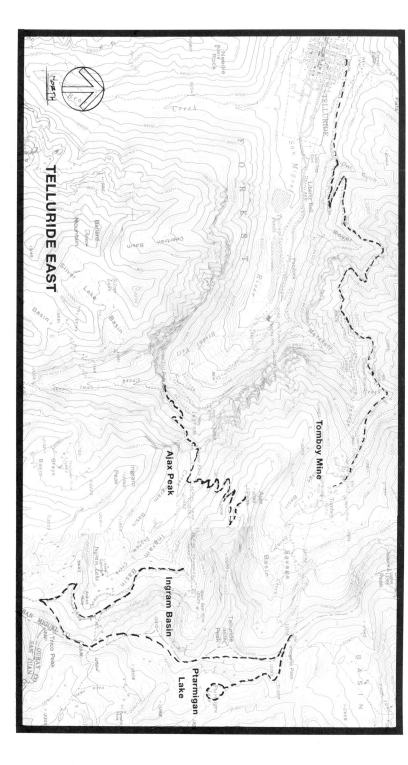

TELLURIDE EAST

43 AJAX PEAK

Time:	**3 1/2 to 4 hours round trip from the road at the power plant**
Distance:	**Approximately 2 1/2 miles**
Elevation Gain:	**2,785 feet**
Maximum Elevation:	**12,785 feet**
Difficulty:	**Difficult**
Trailhead:	**Bridal Veil Falls one way road to Ingram Basin**
Trail End:	**Same as trailhead**
Map:	**U.S.G.S. Telluride Quadrangle**

I had not done this hike before because I thought it was a climb. I'm terrified of heights and I avoid places that require climbing moves or scrambling. Approximately twenty one years ago, my fitness buddy and I were hiking with friends, heading to Imogene Pass from Ingram Basin, and en route some of the group wanted to climb Ajax. From the saddle below Trico, we headed toward Ajax and I found myself walking on places that made me dizzy and uncomfortable. I sat down and waited while the group climbed Ajax and then returned to complete the hike to Imogene Pass.

For years, I looked at that peak from town. My son Scott nearly worshiped Ajax, imagining it to be the tallest mountain in the world, making it the subject of elementary school art projects. It never occurred to me to include Ajax in my book until one reader suggested I add it for its spectacular views. When Nancy Craft told me it was just a hike, I decided to investigate. Several others confirmed Nancy's appraisal, so I got my husband and my youngest son to accompany me on the hike. Indeed, it is a hike, and well worth doing, for the views are riveting. We took photos in every direction, but nothing can do justice to the awe inspiring sights to behold. Do this one as soon as the snow is gone and then do it again before the snow flies. You will not regret it.

Start at the top of Bridal Veil Falls, where the road goes one way to Ingram Falls. It takes about thirty minutes to reach Ingram Falls. The road climbs steeply beyond the falls in the chiseled stone stairs that lead into the basin.

The walk up the road itself is amazing. I marvel at those who find the courage to drive this road. In the early 1970s, you could drive from either direction until one unfortunate couple, driving upward from Bridal Veil Falls, took a tumble in their jeep. One member of the couple was beheaded. From then on, the road was one way. Beware of rock fall, which can be inadvertently set off by cars from above. At one time a boardinghouse sat at the edge of the mountain, just below the falls. (See Ingram Basin hike for further information.)

Watch for cables overhead. Between the third and fourth cable you will find the trail to Ajax heading upward. Look for a small tailings pile and begin hiking up directly underneath it. You will eventually find a well-worn trail which zigs to the east of the tailings and then west and above. Views from the trail are incredible. The trail ends on a grassy ridge which divides Ingram Basin from Savage Basin. The unnamed peak to the west offers more incredible views. You can see Ingram Lake, Silver Lake, the ski area, Lone Cone, the La Sal Mountains in Utah, and views in every direction. It feels like a sheer drop to Bridal Veil Falls which is far below.

44 INGRAM BASIN

Time:	**30 minutes from the road at Bridal Veil power plant to Ingram Falls; to the ridge which separates Ingram Basin and the unnamed basin to the east, 2 1/2hours; to Imogene Pass, 4 to 6 hours**
Distance:	**Approximately 8 miles from the road at Bridal Veil power plant to Imogene Pass**
Elevation Gain:	**Approximately 3,500 feet from the road at Bridal Veil power plant to Telluride Peak**
Elevations:	**10,000 feet at Bridal Veil power plant; 11,000 feet at Ingram Falls; 13,509 feet at Telluride Peak; 13,114 feet at Imogene Pass**
Difficulty:	**Moderate to difficult**
Trailhead:	**Bridal Veil power plant or Imogene Pass**
Trail End:	**Imogene Pass or Bridal Veil power plant**
Map:	**U.S.G.S. Telluride & Ironton Quadrangles**

Be sure to check the weather conditions before you plan your route for this hike. In stormy weather the ridge walk can be exposed to lightning and strong winds. Often snow lingers in this area, making the high traverse above Ptarmigan Lake difficult. It is sometimes advisable to carry an ice axe or to use the alternate lower route, dropping down to the Senator Beck Mine and the road which passes Ptarmigan Lake.

This hike is rich in mining history. If you walk half an hour from the road at the Bridal Veil power plant to Ingram Falls, you will see the ruins of the boardinghouse, home for the miners at the Black Bear stamp mill. The buildings above the road housed a "curve station" for the cable way, and a 20-stamp mill.

The old boardinghouse, situated on the downhill side of the road, was once one of the more spectacular monuments to mining history in the country. Visit the Telluride Museum to see photos of this barn wood beauty where cables were tied to the building to keep this exquisite landmark from blowing off the hill. Careless campers started a fire which engulfed the beautiful old structure and today only photos recapture its romantic past.

The tragic loss of this building illustrates a concern shared by many in opening the back country to recreation. It is imperative that back country travelers observe "No trespassing" signs and beware of potentially danger-ous hazards while being sensitive to the fragile fragments of the area's historic past.

Due to the dangerous road conditions surrounding Ingram Falls, traffic is routed into Telluride, one way only, from the Red Mountain side. Just above Ingram Falls there is a steep, rocky, staircase climb into the basin with spectacular views. Foot travel seems safer than vehicular travel in this area. As you pass under tramway cables, imagine miners riding in ore buckets, seeking safer winter travel than on the avalanche prone roads. If the town bound miners didn't ride the breath-taking tram cross legged on top of the ore, they rode a broad bladed scoop shovel, with the handle in front of them, between their legs, soaring down a series of jumps on rugged terrain, enduring the uncomfortable friction-induced heat.

It is about an hour and a half walk and a 1,325 foot elevation gain to the point on the road passing the fenced off Black Bear Mine. This mine was discovered in 1894 and operated intermittently until 1934. Respect the "No trespassing" signs and don't go inside. Today, this portal offers ventilation for the Idarado Mine. In its early history, the Black Bear Mine was worked mostly by the Finns.

Some incredible slide paths, commonly known as "Finn Boy" or "Fin-lander Slide," parallel the stream coming out of Ingram Basin. The mountain-side can cut loose and cause tremendous damage. In the late 1880s, a fourteen month old boy was found alive after the second story and roof of his house settled down when the first story had been taken out by an avalanche.

"Black Bear miners didn't quit as early as those at other mines. There wasn't any place to go, anyway," said Don O'Rourke, who did a little of everything at that mine. "The tram only ran there when they had enough ore to make it worthwhile, so the younger men often skied to town and waited until the tram ran to ride back up. The men skied in the basin there for something to do."

At 2:00 a.m., Good Friday, April 2, 1927, an avalanche smashed the Black Bear boardinghouse taking the lives of Ed and Marie Rajala, asleep on the bottom floor. She was the cook, and he was the mine operator. Don

O'Rourke, who was in town at that time, had left his clothes in his room on the third story of the boardinghouse. When a second snow slide destroyed the second floor where Harry Thompson slept, he groveled through the debris, finding Don's clothes, dressed in them and went to town for help. When Don saw Harry wearing his clothes, he knew there was an emergency. A few days later, Walt Snodgrass, who "could smell a dead person," found Ed and Marie in their bed with their arms around each other without the covers ruffled.

Further up this road, at 12,000 feet, is Ingram Lake, once known as Lake Constantine. The road continues to a small pond or tarn above, and on to Mineral Basin and Red Mountain Pass. In the scree below Trico Peak, there is a sharp switchback to the left of the main road which heads toward a rocky outcrop separating Ingram Basin and the unnamed basin to the east where the ridge walk to Imogene Pass is found. It takes approximately two and a half hours to this point from the road at the Bridal Veil power plant.

There is a faint road on the east side of this ridge, sometimes interrupted by snow. This spectacular ridge walk is comfortably wide, with no dramatically dangerous or frightening drops. However, the road is intermittent and you will need to look carefully to continue on this route. Bring an ice axe to traverse the snowy sections, as snow often lingers in the summer. Depending on weather and snow and your own preferences, you can take the alternate route from here, dropping down to the Senator Beck Mine or continuing to the unnamed peak. If you chose the high route, you will walk two to three hundred feet below the unnamed, 13,510 foot peak and Telluride Peak. (Ascending each of these peaks in fair weather conditions is an easy walk, well worth the effort.) As you traverse above Ptarmigan Lake, keep heading left, north, where the intermittent road continues to Fort Peabody, or drop down to Ptarmigan Lake and use the jeep road beyond the lake to the pass.

Ingram Lake

In 1903, the State Militia occupied Fort Peabody to keep strikers out of Savage and Marshall basins. Imagine them close to freezing with a 360 degree view of the San Juan Mountains. What determination strikebreakers must have had to risk their lives in these extremely remote and rugged mountains.

I love this hike. The ridge walk is comfortable and the views are fabulous. Keep your eyes open for crystals on the ridge en route to Ptarmigan Lake.

45 PTARMIGAN LAKE

Time:	1/2 hour to **Ptarmigan Lake** from **Imogene Pass**; 3 hours from **Bridal Veil** power plant
Distance:	Approximately 1/2 mile to **Ptarmigan Lake** from **Imogene Pass**; 2 miles from **Ingram Basin**
Elevation Gain:	Drop 400 feet from **Imogene Pass** to **Ptarmigan Lake**; approximately 900 feet gain from **Ingram Basin**
Maximum Elevation:	13,200 feet
Difficulty:	Easy from **Imogene Pass** to **Ptarmigan Lake**; Moderate from **Ingram Basin**
Trailhead:	The top of **Bridal Veil Falls**, or at **Imogene Pass**
Trail End:	Imogene Pass, or at Bridal Veil Falls
Map:	U.S.G.S. Ironton Quadrangle and Telluride Quadrangle

You can walk to Ptarmigan Lake from Ingram Basin (see Ingram Basin hike for directions) or from Imogene Pass above Savage Basin (see Tomboy Mine directions).

You can drive a 4-wheel drive vehicle to Ptarmigan Lake on the jeep road from Imogene Pass. From the ridge at Imogene Pass, you can see Red Mountain and the 180 degree views are spectacular.

Take a lunch and picnic if you are going to Ptarmigan Lake. It is a scenic place to relax among artifacts of mining history. Ptarmigan Lake is at 12,939 feet. Six smaller lakes are very close by and several old wooden buildings are still standing. Ptarmigan is directly west of Telluride Peak; it is a short drop over the ridge from Imogene Pass. The Camp Bird Mine vein goes through the middle of the lake.

This hike should include a visit to Fort Peabody as well. This is a beautiful area, and the mining relics to be found spark the imagination.

At one time, Ptarmigan Lake was the only source of water for Savage Basin. A man had to be there at all times to keep the pumps operating. "Whispering" Jim Dalpez watched the pumps there for four dollars a day, plus food and reading material. Jimmy thought he had a good deal for two years in the early 1920s when he lived there with tomcats. He had a phone and he snowshoed back and forth from the Tomboy Mine once or twice a month.

After the first snowfall one winter, ptarmigans ate from his hand on the porch. When one of his tomcats wanted to pounce on the ptarmigan, Jim hit

Ptarmigan Lake

him with a broom. No one ever visited Jim up there, but he got along just fine with all he could read and the tomcats.

Jim spent fifty years in the mines. He is of Austrian descent and in addition to English, he speaks five languages: French, Italian, Spanish, German, and Austrian. He remembers being made fun of by local kids because of his parents' accent. He drank a lot of whiskey, worked ten hours a day, read Zane Grey novels, and had a variety of accidents. Once when he was a boss in the mine, he was buried with one boot sticking out. He dislocated his shoulder, but he still went to work the next day with his arm in a sling. Jim is but one example of the many devotional employees of the mining era.

46 TOMBOY MINE

Time:	**2 hours to the Tomboy Mine, another hour to Imogene Pass**
Distance:	**5 miles to the Tomboy Mine**
Elevation Gain:	**2,300 feet**
Maximum Elevation:	**13,385 feet**
Difficulty:	**Difficult**
Trailhead:	**Tomboy Road and Oak Street**
Trail End:	**Same as trailhead**
Map:	**U.S.G.S. Telluride Quadrangle**

The Tomboy Mine is located in Savage Basin, a glacial cirque in which the road levels out at about 11,500 feet. The valley was once bustling with the activity of 2,000 people occupying about 100 houses, a large sixty-stamp mill, livery stables, a school, machine shops, a store, a three-story boarding-house, a movie theater, a bowling alley, tennis courts, and a YMCA.

The walk to Tomboy from Telluride is straightforward and obvious. You walk on the jeep road which goes northeast from town, gaining 2,300 feet from town to Savage Basin. The hike to Tomboy Mine is best when the traffic is minimal.

Whether you walk, bike, or drive, Savage Basin and the Tomboy Mine are important links with Telluride and a must to see. Visit our local museum to see photos of the basin when the mines were in operation and the area was heavily populated.

In the early 1900s, a horse ride from Telluride to Savage Basin was three hours. The first waterfall in Owl Gulch was a popular horse watering stop for miners who had their own saddle horses. Once they arrived at work, the miners tied the reins around the saddle horn and the horse went back to the barn in town by itself.

On the way, you will pass the Allegheny Mine site where there is a wooden fence to keep out trespassers. Continue walking up the steep switchback to the west and then the road flattens, heading east into Royer Gulch, where the falls flow in the spring and early summer. Views of Ingram and Bridal Veil Falls from this area are impressive. Continue beyond Royer Gulch to the rock tunnel commonly known as "Social Tunnel" from which views of Telluride are spectacular. "Social Tunnel" was blasted for access to the mining discoveries in Savage and Marshall Basins.

Continue walking past the Cimarron Mine, located just before the road crosses Marshall Creek. In this area there are still many collapsed old wooden remnants of the area's rich history.

Between Marshall and Savage Basins is an avalanche area known as "Elephant Slide." This was also a "neutral" zone between the Smuggler and the Tomboy mines called the "Jungle," where prostitutes operated. This slide killed men who lived in the Smuggler boardinghouse as they walked to work at Tomboy.

Once heavily forested, the basin around the Tomboy Mine, discovered in 1880 and closed in 1927, is nearly barren. Most of the canyons, gulches, and basins in the Tomboy region have been mined. Many tree stumps are visible in Savage Basin, where most of the old wood buildings have been weathered, burned, or pilfered. The rock structures are somewhat in tact. Where the cribbing still exists, the first stamp mill stood. Approximately one-half mile up the basin, there is a rock structure which was once the powder house, used to protect explosives.

Barns, beer halls, and boardinghouses dotted the area where steep and precarious trails hung over the mountainsides. The communities, town-ships, and brotherhoods formed in these high mountain cirques were testimony to the hardy inhabitants who walked these hills. T.A. Pickard, in *Across the San Juan Mountains*, wrote:

"In southwest Colorado, where the mountain slopes are steep and but poorly protected by forests, there are more people killed each year from snow slides than in Switzerland, although the man of leisure who risks his life climbing the Swiss heights usually receives more mention in the daily press than the miners and other humble individuals that lost their lives in the San Juan while going to and from their labor."

Single men of many nationalities stayed at the boardinghouse on the edge of Savage Basin. They were Swedes, Finns, and Slavs, known as "bull hunks." The "bull hunks" were big men. As Jim Dalpez, a pump watcher at Ptarmigan Lake in the 1920s put it, "They wasn't no peanut jobs."

In those days, miners did not work at one place long, and they carried their bedrolls from boardinghouse to boardinghouse. Bedbugs were a terrible problem at the boardinghouse at the Tomboy Mine because miners' bedrolls were often unwashed. There were fifty rooms with four men in each room. When one room at a time was fumigated, the bugs moved from room to room. Miners put the bed legs in cans of kerosene to keep away the bugs, but they just moved to the ceilings where they simply dropped on beds from above.

Everything was in snow sheds at Tomboy. People could live a whole winter without putting their feet in the snow. They had to shovel snow daily, but children missed very few days of school. One old timer remembers shoveling snow then walking half a mile to attend the first grade up there in 1915.

One year, families living in Savage Basin made bootleg whiskey out of raisins. People were astonished at the raisin consumption when large quantities of raisins were delivered. The water was drawn from springs, about ten feet below the surface, until February. There was a big tank that held about 200 gallons of water with an electric heater in it. They often had to shovel snow for water as well.

Once a month there was a dance and the miners hired stages to bring the women from town to dance. There was no shortage of men, who had to walk to the dances. Occasionally, mine employees had the privilege of riding the tram to town. Telluride Transfer had a horse barn in town and it was a $2.00 round trip horse ride to Tomboy.

Harry Wright operated the junction house in Savage Basin while working for Western Colorado Power. He worked almost 24 hours a day, seven days a week for $87.50 a month. In those days, the water was so pure that Harry had to add salt to conduct electricity. Earlier, he ran the locomotive and took ore out of the mine. Harry and his fellow workers would earn a one dollar bonus if they made eleven trips. Harry remembers the sometimes scary ride in the tram bucket to the boardinghouse.

Above the ruins in Savage Basin, the nearly 2,000 foot climb to Imogene Pass takes about an hour. On the pass is a shelter, Fort Peabody, which was

Tomboy (courtesy Don O'Rourke)

built by the militia to guard against the strikers' return to the area. Up the rocky ridge to the south, right, is a stone sentry building. From the pass the road continues left to Yankee Boy Basin and Ouray, or right to Ptarmigan Lake, linking with Black Bear Pass and Ingram Basin.

The Tomboy Road to Ouray is usually open about ten weeks out of the year, from July through early September. Below, to the north, is Camp Bird where the road crosses Sneffels Creek and continues right to Ouray. If you plan to hike to Ouray, it is a good idea to plant a car or to have someone pick you up at the Camp Bird Mine. It is highly recommended to end the day in Ouray's hot springs pool, a treat worth the work to enjoy after this full day's walk.

The Tomboy Road is also the route for the Imogene Pass Run, done yearly the weekend after Labor Day. It is an eighteen mile run from Ouray to Telluride and runners are frequently rained, snowed, or hailed upon at the top of the pass. The fastest runners make it in a little more than two hours.

┌─ **47** GALLOPING GOOSE ─┐

Time:	I hour
Distance:	**Approximately 3 I/2 miles**
Elevation Gain:	**Approximately 200 feet**
Maximum Elevation:	**8,600 feet**
Difficulty:	**Easy**
Trailhead:	**Ilium church camp**
Trail End:	**Ames power plant**
Maps:	**U.S.G.S. Gray Head and Mount Wilson quadrangles**

To do the section from the Ilium church camp to the Ames power plant by itself is a wonderful short historic stroll. This is a flat walk which goes along the old railroad grade. You will see railroad ties, some still in place, and some stacked by the side of the trail. Where the walls have been reinforced, there was a trestle high above the valley. You will pass through talus slopes, where rock froze and thawed and then fell from the cliffs above. You will have spectacular views of the Ophir Needles as you walk below the site of the Ice Hose, a winter ice climb. This trail is primarily used as a bicycle path, but it is a great walk for those with bad knees, unacclimatized, and out of shape for the steep climbs of most hikes in the area.

The Galloping Goose Trail utilizes portions of the abandoned Rio Grande Southern Railroad grade from Lawson Hill to Lizard Head Pass. The Rio Grande Southern traveled 162 miles from Ridgway over Dallas Divide to Placerville, to Telluride and Ophir, over Lizard Head Pass to Rico, through Dolores and Mancos, and on to Durango where a connection with the Denver and Rio Grande was made. Financial problems and lack of road bed maintenance threw the line into receivership.

The first Galloping Goose came out of the depot in Ridgway in 1931 and, despite difficulties, kept Otto Mears' narrow gauge railroad running in the mountains of Southwest Colorado.

The Galloping Goose rail bus ran on the rail line from the 1930s to 1951. There were eight Geese built using Pierce Arrow or Buick engines. Number 4 resides in Telluride, next to the San Miguel County Courthouse. Auto engines powered with gasoline were used, and a sedan car seat was widened to accommodate ten passengers, with a trailer body to haul freight. Some old timers who rode the Goose from Ridgway to Telluride remember the sound of the clackety, clack, which resembled the honk of a goose and scared animals off the track.

Phase 1 of the reconstruction of the trail for recreational use is nearly

Galloping Goose

complete. Starting at Lawson Hill, the trail runs along portions of the San Miguel River and then to Ilium where it continues downhill to the Ilium church camp and crosses the South Fork, heads up the Sunshine Mesa road and connects with the railroad grade again, running south above South Fork. At the present time, the improved trail ends by the Ames hydroelectric power plant, just below the Ophir Loop where the railroad utilized a series of trestles to negotiate the steep grade from Ophir to Telluride.

The Ames Station was one of the world's first hydroelectric stations. The plant generates electricity with the pressure created by water carried in pipes from Trout Lake. One of the biggest problems in operating the plant was the lightning strikes. The operators developed a lightning arrester, a tub of salt water which grounded the power lines. One day, lightning struck while a bull drank out of the tub. The bull died by electrocution. "That's no bull," one old timer joked.

—**48** ICE LAKE BASIN—

Time:	**1 hour and 15 minutes to lower Ice Lake Basin; 2 hours to Ice Lake**
Distance:	**Approximately 2 miles to lower Ice Lake Basin; 3 miles to Ice Lake**
Elevation Gain:	**Approximately 1,200 feet to lower Ice Lake Basin; 2,400 feet to Ice Lake**
Maximum Elevation:	**12,585 feet at Fuller Lake**
Difficulty:	**Moderate**
Trailhead:	**South Mineral Creek Campground**
Trail End:	**Same as trailhead**
Map:	**U.S.G.S. Ophir Quadrangle**

Ice Lake Basin is a popular summer hiking area. (See map on pages 14-15.) It is best to go during the week to avoid the crowds. From Telluride, the quickest route to the trailhead is to drive over Ophir Pass to Red Mountain Highway and turn right, south, toward Silverton, to the South Mineral Creek Campground road. You will drive past several designated campgrounds to the South Mineral Creek Campground. It takes about an hour and a half to drive from Telluride to the trailhead across the road from the South Mineral Creek Campground.

It is an hour and fifteen minutes of continuous uphill walking through a pine forest to lower Ice Lake Basin. This meadowland offers meditative sites for reflection as well as challenging rock walls for intrepid climbers. The trail continues another thousand feet uphill, for another hour, up to Ice Lake, above tree line where meadows are bursting with wildflowers

Ice Lake

and meandering streams. Pilot Knob, Golden Horn, and U.S. Grant Peaks tower above a handful of easily accessible lakes.

This alpine wonderland can also be reached from Hope Lake and Waterfall Canyon in Ophir for those looking for more challenge.

༄

49 LAKE HOPE

Time:	**Plan on 1 1/2 hours from the trailhead to the lake, 3 hours round trip.**
Distance:	**5.3 miles round trip**
Elevation Gain:	**1,900 feet**
Maximum Elevation:	**11,880 feet**
Difficulty:	**Moderate**
Trailhead:	**2 1/2 miles north of Trout Lake on Hidden Lakes Road #627. Follow the road around Trout Lake for 1 mile and turn left at the junction with the Hidden Lakes road. Go 2 1/2 miles to the parking area and trailhead sign.**
Trail End:	**Same as trailhead**
Map:	**U.S.G.S. Ophir Quadrangle**
Forest Service Trail:	**#410**

This hike is a favorite among locals and visitors. (See map on Page 90.) The route to Lake Hope is found from Trout Lake. Take Highway #145 from Telluride to Trout Lake and take the Trout Lake Road #626 to #627, turning left, north, at the Y. Drive approximately fifteen minutes to the Lake Hope trailhead, #410 and park.

The trail is gradual, winding up through the trees for the first forty-five minutes. Cross two streams; at the third, go left, to the 2nd crossing. Look up to your left at the rust colored scree field that looks like tailings, and wind up through the forest on the left, west, side of a rock walled creek bed. You have approximately forty minutes of fairly steep walking ahead to reach the lake, which you won't see until you are there. Notice Trout Lake and Vermilion Peak as you climb. At the end of the lake, to the west, note San Miguel Peak, where winter helicopter skiing is sometimes accessed Behind you, to the northeast, notice Vermilion Peak to the left above the red shale. Beattie Peak is just to the left, east, of the lake.

Lake Hope

Take caution and leave early to avoid lightning which often accompanies summer rain and thunderstorms. Distances are deceptive up here. Plan on walking about two miles an hour, but know that altitude takes its toll and allow for extra time. Notice Sheep Mountain and Lizard Head as you walk approximately one hour and fifteen minutes down.

This area was once sheep grazed. To the south are two small unnamed lakes. At one time stocked with fish by the power company, Lake Hope is a wonderful place to see wildflowers. It is a natural lake which was used to supplement Trout Lake in storing water for the Ames power plant. At one time the lake was drained by overflow and later a tunnel was driven under the lake to control the drainage. A caretaker stayed there year round and had to snowshoe to leave. He had a telephone line fixed so he could communicate. Surrounded by dramatically sharp peaks above 13,000 feet, it can be a good fishing spot. Depending on the power needs, the lake can be full or low.

In the 1960s, Bill Bray ran sheep under Yellow Mountain to Lake Hope. He had to move his camps each week to keep the sheep from overgrazing. The camps had ten by ten, four-foot walled tents which they had to move on pack horses and mules. Sometimes bear killed the sheep.

50 PRIEST LAKES

Time:	1/2 hour to walk around the lake
Distance:	Less than 1/2 mile
Elevation Gain:	None
Maximum Elevation:	9,568 feet
Difficulty:	Easy
Trailhead:	Highway 145 south to the Trout Lake turnoff; take the first left heading north less than 3/4 mile to Priest Lakes
Trail End:	Same as trailhead
Map:	Trails Illustrated Topo 141, Silverton, Ouray, Telluride, Lake City; U.S.G.S. Mount Wilson Quadrangle

These are man-made lakes named after the Priest brothers who lived at Matterhorn, the present San Bernardo. At one time Matterhorn had a big saloon, ladies of the night, and many houses, above which people cut cord wood which never got hauled out. The railroad went on the road to Priest Lakes where an old wooden flume paralleled the road. Flume walkers were hired to check the condition of the flume. Two old cabins sit on either side of the lake. At one time, fishermen were required to pay for the amount of fish they caught.

Walk around the lake on an old roadbed and trail. Fishing here can be good and the camp sites are lovely. This is an advanced-years walk for the "mature."

Priest Lakes

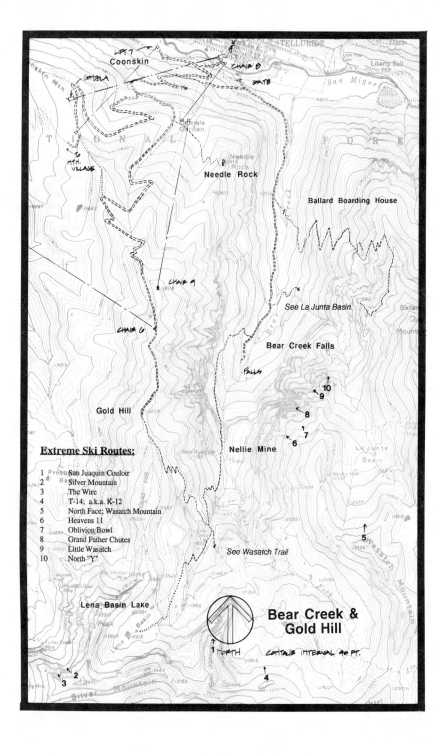

Extreme Ski Routes:

1 San Juaquin Couloir
2 Silver Mountain
3 The Wire
4 T-14; a.k.a. K-12
5 North Face; Wasatch Mountain
6 Heavens 11
7 Oblivion Bowl
8 Grand Father Chutes
9 Little Wasatch
10 North "Y"

Bear Creek &
Gold Hill

51 SKI AREA

Skiing around Telluride was initially a Scandinavian utilitarian activity providing travel from the mines. Today, it provides an economic foundation five months a year to help support the local economy. In an area of once rugged and unrestricted individualism, opinions about ski area development are diverse. Those in favor of expansion are juxtaposed to those who favor restraint. Everyone agrees on one aspect however, the exhilaration, the beauty, and the views are remarkable beyond comparison.

In the 1960s, the town built a rope tow at the top of the "Kids' Hill," which is the bottom of what is now the Plunge. Then the mountain was heavily logged to provide building materials for mining. In the winter of 1972-73, the ski area opened with five lifts. No lifts serviced the front of the mountain. In those years skiers hiked from the top of lift #6 to the top of Bushwhacker or the Plunge. Skiing to town on the front of the mountain was often the last run of the day as access to the bottom was a long ordeal of riding around in a vehicle and taking four lifts back up to the top again.

Today, new lifts, added runs, advances in ski equipment and skier abilities have created a whole new experience for the Telluride skier. To hike on the ski area in the summer offers a whole new perspective. Take a look at what is available and get up there for another view of town and an appreciation of this winter wonderland.

Here are some places to see on the ski area:
>Coonskin
>Needle Rock
>Gold Hill
>Lena Basin
>Double Cabins

Old logging and mining roads and new ski area maintenance roads offer relatively easy hiking and biking, scenic byways throughout the ski area and the Mountain Village. Homesteaders settled much of Turkey Creek Mesa and the area is rich in historical lore. Most of the ski runs were named after mining claims and have stories worth repeating. Like hiking in the Wilderness Area, you are discouraged from bringing dogs which disturb wildlife on the ski area. Motorcycles are not permitted, as they tear up the trails too much. However, bicycles are allowed on the ski area trails.

Go at your own risk and pay attention. There are a number of access points to the ski area. The following are some of the ways to begin your exploration:

Coonskin chair lift #7

The Gondola

Bear Creek: Hike up the Wasatch Trail beyond the Nellie Mine to Gold Hill and the top of lifts #6 and #9.

Mountain Village: There are old logging and ski area maintenance roads which lead up to Gorrono and See Forever.

Here are some of the places of interest on the ski area:

Camel's Garden: This area below lift #9 is a meadow where a summer vegetable garden provided tasty delights to be sold in town. At one time, there were four cabins where two inch pipes conducted water to each cabin.

Milk Farm: This is the flat area where Coonskin and Milk Run meet. A Finlander kept a couple of cows there and sold the milk in town.

Gorrono: This area was first homesteaded by the McDonald family. Woodrow Wilson signed the homestead documents. Gorrono, named after the second family who lived there, was given to the site to avoid confusion with the popular fast food chain. T. J. McDonald held the documents on Gorrono from September 22, 1887 to January 21, 1901. Mouse McDonald remembers that his grandfather served on the Union side in the Civil War. Mouse still treasures his grandfather's discharge papers and the cap and ball gun he used in the Civil War. Mouse walked to school from the log cabins built by his grandfather, still standing at Gorrono, to San Miguel (Telluride's original town site across from the Boomerang Road on Highway 145) where he attended a one room school. The building housing the ski school was once a barn for cows and horses. The saloon was a home. The small building, now in severe disrepair, was a hay barn. All the trees were cut out of the area in 1925. In 1942, Robert King bought approximately 900 acres from Tim Murray McDonald, Mouse's dad, and eventually sold out to the Gorronos who ran sheep there in the summer. In October of 1968, Joe Zoline bought the acreage to develop the Telluride Ski Area. Snowmobiles went up to Camel's Garden, the Power Line and the North Chute to provide skiing before the lifts opened in the winter of 1972-73.

Double Cabins: Old timer Harry Wright built the two cabins there with his step father. They used one of the cabins to store wood and lived in the other. Harry walked to attend school at the one room schoolhouse in San Miguel when he was a kid.

౩౧

52 COONSKIN

Time:	**It is about a 1 1/2 hour walk from the bottom of Coonskin Lift to the top.**
Distance:	**Approximately 3 miles round trip**
Elevation Gain:	**Approximately 1,700 feet**
Maximum Elevation:	**Approximately 10,400 feet**
Difficulty:	**Moderate**
Trailhead:	**Bottom of Lift #7, lower Plunge**
Trail End:	**Top of Lift #7, on See Forever**
Map:	**U.S.G.S. Telluride Quadrangle**

Before the snow falls and the ski area is open, it is a good aerobic walk to hike up the front of the mountain to the top of Lift #7. The top of Coonskin Mountain is 10,600 feet, and the nearly 2,000 foot ascent is breathtaking. The walk is continuously steep on the Telluride Trail, primarily a road. This is a good, short workout and a great training run or walk to get in shape for the ski season soon to come.

This mountain was named after an old Ute Indian legend. As the chill of fall creeps into the air, so too appears the broken outline of the coonskin, spread across the lower Plunge. Some view this outline as verification of an old Indian curse cast upon the valley. It may, on the other hand, represent the hopes and dreams manifested in the hearts of man inhabiting the valley. The story of the coonskin is repeated each fall.

One Indian brave shot his arrow at a raccoon and wounded him. The animal, terrified and in pain, rushed around dripping blood from his fatal wound, and crawled on and on, finally staggering, falling, and dying. The aspens quivered with sorrow as they watched the innocent animal's blood fertilize their roots.

When the Indian brave found his dead prey, he skinned the raccoon and made a cap out of his fur. As the aspens mourned the loss of the dead animal, the trees pay tribute to his memory each fall. Their leaves turn color, outlining the shape of the raccoon's skin.

The head lies on the northwest (right side in photo), with the legs outstretched and the tail to the southeast, just like a whole raccoon skin stretched out to dry and cure.

Each year the first yellow leaves to appear on the aspens take the shape of the raccoon, following the trail his wounded body's blood spread throughout the forest.

The story continues that in the next year, seeing the forest in mourning, the band of Indians fled from the area and the young brave, overcome by a

Coonskin as outlined in the fall

great melancholy, took his own life.

Old museum photos may contradict the accuracy of this legend. In the early 1900s there were no trees on this front hillside. First to regenerate are the aspens, then the spruce and then the fir.

Watch the colors change across the mountain in the early fall and look for the outline of the coonskin. It can best be seen from the Jud Wiebe as you look across the valley.

✈

53 GOLD HILL

Time:	**3 1/2 to 5 hours to the top of Gold Hill**
Distance:	**Approximately 4.9 miles to the top of Gold Hill**
Elevation Gain:	**Approximately 3,560 feet**
Maximum Elevation:	**12,320 Feet**
Difficulty:	**Difficult**
Trailhead:	**Bottom of Lift #7 or Bear Creek Road**
Trail End:	**Same as trailhead**
Map:	**U.S.G.S. Telluride Quadrangle**

At the top of gold Hill, the views are awe-inspiring. You get a feel for ski area expansion plans and a sense of the profound as you take time to enjoy the breathtaking panorama.

You can get to Gold Hill from Bear Creek (see Nellie Mine and Lena Basin Lake) or by walking up See Forever to the top of Lift #6. From the Nellie Mine continue upstream staying right, west, of the creek. Soon after passing the mine, the road climbs steeply away and takes a sharp right. Walk on a well-defined, old wagon road to the top of the ski area. While walking up this road, watch for stunted and full purple Indian paintbrush and a few white columbine high on the trail.

This is a straightforward hike with spectacular 180-degree views at the top: the La Sal Mountains of southeast Utah, Lizard Head, the Wilsons, the town of Telluride, and Lone Cone. Other prominent features include La Junta Basin, the Ballard Boardinghouse, Wasatch Mountain, La Junta Peak, Ballard Mountain, and St. Sophia Ridge.

From the top of the road at the top of Lift #6 to Gold Hill, it is possible to walk into Lena Basin, directly south, or to ascend Gold Hill for more lofty views. You can also stay high on the ridge and view the lake in Lena Basin from above. The views of Alta Lakes and Prospect Basin are incredible from this ridge. It takes about an hour to walk to the top of the ridge from the high point on the road. It is more direct (and strenuous) to scramble up to the ridge before the road reaches the top.

Several descents are possible from the top of the road to Gold Hill. You

From Gold Hill to Lena Basin

can walk right, to the north, down the ski area. This is a four-mile descent from the top of Gold Hill into town. Probably the fastest route is about a two-hour walk down See Forever to the Telluride Trail to town. For a contrast of mining and ski mountain perspectives, and a view of the front of the mountain without snow, this descent is interesting. Another return is to go into Lena Basin and walk back down Bear Creek.

For an interesting, full-day adventure, spectacular sights, and a re-minder of Telluride's historical heritage, follow the echos of the past and walk up Gold Hill. Gold Hill was aptly named for its rich veins and was once one of the richest mining areas in the world, producing fourteen ounces of gold per ton. The gold content there was supposedly twenty times that of Ouray, and many diggings are still visible.

54 NEEDLE ROCK

Time:	**It is about 1 1/2 hours from the Coonskin parking area to the top of the ridge where Needle Rock sits. Plan on at least 3 hours for this round trip.**
Distance:	**Less than 1 mile**
Elevation Gain:	**Approximately 1,856 feet**
Maximum Elevation:	**10,656 feet**
Difficulty:	**Difficult (The last leg of the hike is extremely difficult.)**
Trailhead:	**Bottom of the Coonskin lift**
Trail End:	**Same as trailhead**
Map:	**U.S.G.S. Telluride Quadrangle**

Needle Rock is an exciting place to be. The views are unique, but be prepared because the brush is thick and there really isn't a true trail. Start at the bottom of Coonskin and walk up the Telluride Trail. Where the Milk Farm crosses the trail, take the road that continues east (to the left) to Camel's Garden.

Camel's Garden is the last rest stop before either riding back up Lift #9 or skiing the lower Plunge. It's a nice meadow, albeit in the rainy season filled with flies and other nastily biting insects. Go prepared with bug repellent if you are hiking during the rainy summer season.

The trail to Needle Rock is a little used footpath, very overgrown, hard to follow, and often non-existent. It is just left of Lift #9 and follows the ridge to the rock. There may be a lot of bushwhacking on this hike, so wear old clothes and be prepared to scrape and tear them as you climb through the trees. There are many hints of game, and a faint footpath which you can follow first in one direction and then the other, ultimately scrambling through branches and over logs. (It isn't much of a trail.) As the ridge steepens, you may scramble on loose rock. At that point, you are most likely directly below Needle Rock.

From the ridge below Needle Rock, the view of town is dramatic. You will see a hole in the rock, which may have been the "eye of the needle." Behind the largest rock is "Pin Rock," so called by old timers. Stay away from the Bear Creek side where there are many steep drop-offs and cliffs. Return to Camel's Garden the way you came up.

The hike down is pretty much like the ascent. Just be sure to keep left as you descend, staying clear of the red cliffs below. It is about 45 minutes back down to Camel's Garden. It is about a three hour round trip for in-shape locals on this undefined trail.

Needle Rock looms proudly over town. Its presence on the horizon has attracted much curiosity. The Finlanders first put the pole and the flag atop the rock. Later, ski patrollers climbed it and flags were hung for hang glider pilots to gauge wind directions.

An old timer told me about the trail up the ridge from Camel's Garden. Mr. Camel grew beautiful vegetables there which he brought to town to sell each summer.

There are also stories about many years ago when people were very poor. They planted a pot of money below Needle Rock and two teams of men raced to the top for the "pot of gold." Today, there is no pot of gold, but if you're lucky you may find yourself near the end of a rainbow.

Needle Rock

55 EXTREME SKIS

For nearly nine months a year, winter's white coat covers the gurgling streams, the grasses, and the brown dirt on the ski area. In the winter, while the ski area is open, I ride the lifts daydreaming of summertime places to hike, enjoying the views of the peaks and the tiny dollhouse town below with the stark contrast of blue skies in the crisp, cool, invigorating air. While I love to ski, I truly enjoy being on the ski area in the summer, walking through the green grass and fragrant flowers, remembering winter's adventures.

Some take skiing to the extreme, looking for adrenaline and audacious experiences that to others is fool hearty. At the top of lift #9, looking left, east, across Bear Creek to the rocky cliffs is a series of steep chutes that I wouldn't consider hiking, let alone skiing. Such couloirs are more commonly tracked in European alpine villages. These provided the stimulus for the first recorded descents in the Telluride region where risk- takers ventured into the back country, beyond ski area safety, despite the notorious propensity of San Juan Mountain avalanches. (It is illegal to access these adventures through the ski area, but if someone wants to risk his own life without endangering others, away from the Forest Serviced land, it is his individual choice.)

Andy Sawyer is one whose exploits take away my breath. One of his outrageous alpine adventures was inspired by a friend who had recently returned from France, and shared stories of European alpine adventurism. While I enjoyed skiing the groomed corduroy of Bushwhacker one morning, Andy was across the canyon, rappelling off his ski, skiing a chute of 55 degrees in the only descent ever recorded of what he called "Heaven's 11," an impossible and insane looking route on the ridge commonly called "Little Wasatch."

For one who gets a thrill from the sunrise and sunset experiences, I can barely imagine even thinking of the possibilities that Andy dares to consider, but I truly enjoy looking, appreciating someone else's high adventure. (Keep in mind that these experiences are very serious, even to those who participate. The snow conditions vary considerably, and you are completely on your own, far away from rescue. Serious injury and death can easily occur. Remember that access through the ski area is forbidden by law.) For your perspective and appreciation, I'm including a few of these feats to embellish the landscape as you hike. These are numbered as indicated on the accompanying map on page 130.

1. San Joaquin Ridge: Standing at the top of lift #6 or #9 this ridge runs north and south, dividing Lena Basin and upper Bear Creek. The steep snow chute, which chokes down, requiring fast turns, is a super serious ski, 12-14 feet wide, averaging just under fifty degrees. This was first skied by Dennis and Kevin Green and Hugh Sawyer. It is a classic extreme ski today,

one of the most commonly done extreme skis in the area, where more than one broken femur has resulted. This chute is prone to slide. Andy took an avalanche ride once, and, fortunately, doing the elementary back stroke, he swam out of it alive.

2. Silver Mountain: Andy and Surfer Dan made the first recorded descents of this.

3. The Wire: Andy soloed this one. Skiing this was a major step-up in the local extreme ski world, opening doors, pushing past limits. Andy used a technique called "stemming," with his hands and his feet twisted out, then launching off the bulge of rock in the middle of this one. He landed on his edges and "self-arrested," a technique used to stop a steep fall.

4. T14: This unofficially named peak is at the head of Bear Creek. This is a route from Ophir to Telluride.

5. Wasatch Mountain: This is a long, all day adventure. The ski is more moderate than the other extreme skis identified. From the north face of this mountain, you can ski down Bear Creek.

6. Heaven's 11: After making the only descent ever, Andy doubts he'll ever repeat this one. He describes this as "most incredible." This route was done unplanned; it was a complete accident. Early one March, Andy talked to Neil Ringstad, who had just returned from France. Neil told Andy about how the French had rappelled into ski routes. Andy went up there alone, just to look, giving himself a turn around time. After stopping for lunch, Andy traversed across to take a closer look. He could see into the chute that the snow conditions and the light, everything, was perfect, while he was separated from the route by a 20-25 foot vertical cliff. (That's the dark rock above the chute.) He decided to go for it and, remembering the information Neil had shared about the French, he applied a never before tried technique, using his ski to rappel off. People on the ski area were lined up, watching, as Andy rappelled down to the end of his rope, landing at the top of a 55 degree chute, 225 cm wide. He felt like he was in real trouble, but, fortunately, his rope technique worked and he pulled his ski down to him. Below was close to a 1,000 feet drop. Andy was on 200 cm. skis, with about four inches on either side of his tip and tail. From across the canyon, Andy had looked at the two chutes and thought to call it "Heaven's 11." He claims that this was more skiable than it looked, adding that in the tighter sections below he had to stick his ski tails into the snow, with his skis sticking straight out, and walked down on his tails, "tail walking," he called it. The Ski Patrol was not alone in witnessing Andy's feat, probably 200 people lined the top of #9 watching in astonishment.

7. Oblivion Bowl: This is the open bowl above and to the left of Heaven's 11, centrally located on the ridge. Andy and Brian O'Neil did the first descent of this one in a total white-out. Andy knew the route only because he had studied it for so long. This bowl arcs down to feed into the next route, the Grand Daddy.

8. Grand Daddy: The discontinuous couloirs going down to the left

of Oblivion Bowl mark this one which was originally done by Neil Ringstad, Lance McDonald, and Andy Sawyer. This is the entire gully system that runs down the whole face.

9. Little Wasatch: From below, looking up Bear Creek, this looks like a separate mountain, but it is really a shoulder of Wasatch Mountain. Andy Sawyer spent three years looking at this from different angles, in different lights and shadows. After the first descent, Andy, Brian O'Neil, Lance McDonald, and Neil Ringstad found this route straightforward and (almost) simple compared to the others they had done. This one was 2,500 feet of vertical, sustained at 40 to 45 degrees. They rappelled off a tree that may not even be there now. To see the Y: look from below Guiseppe's between the top of lifts #9 and #6, coming off the left side of the rock faced ridge across the canyon to your left, northeast.

10. The North Y: On the left side of the rocky shoulder. This one can be seen from the park.

‍ঌ৲

Additional Sources

The following books represent the most useful resources I have found. It is worthwhile to browse through some of these as well as the local library and the museum for more in-depth information about the area.

Backus, Harriet; *Tomboy Bride*

Borneman and Lampert; *A Climber's Guide to Colorado's Fourteeners*

Brown, Robert L.; *Jeep Trails to Colorado Ghost Towns*

Darley, George M.; *Pioneering in the San Juans*

Denison, L.G. and York, L.A.; *Telluride Tales of Two Early Pioneers*

Gibbons, J.J.; *In the San Juans*

Griffiths, Mel, and Rubright, Lynnellt; *Colorado*

Griffiths, Thomas M.; *San Juan Country*

Koch, David; *The Colorado Pass Book*

Lavender, David; *David Lavender's Colorado, One Man's West, The Rockies, A Rocky Mountain Fantasy,* and *The Telluride Story*

Lavender, Dwight and Long, Carlton Curtis and Griffiths, T. Melvin; *The San Juan Mountaineers' Climbers Guide to Southwest Colorado*

Norton, Boyd and Barbara; *Backroads of Colorado*

Ormes, Robert; *Guide to the Colorado Mountains*

Pixler, Paul; *Hiking Trails of Southwest Colorado*

Rickard, T.K.; *Across the San Juans*

Rockwell, Wilson; *The Utes: A Forgotten People*

Rosebrough, Robert F.; *The San Juan Mountains, A Climbing and Hiking Guide*

Rockwell, Wilson; *Uncompahgre Country*

Smith, Duane; *Rocky Mountain Mining Camps*

The Mountaineers, Seattle, Washington; *Mountaineering, The Freedom of the Hills, third ed.*

Wolle, Muriel Sible; *Stampede to Timberline*

Wenger, Martin G.; *Recollections of Telluride Colorado*